BADEN-
THE MAN WHO LIVED TWICE

Baden-Powell:
The Man Who
Lived Twice

by

MARY DREWERY

HODDER AND STOUGHTON
LONDON SYDNEY AUCKLAND TORONTO

Acknowledgments

IN THIS ACCOUNT of Lord Baden-Powell's life, there are many quotations from his letters, articles and books. I have tried to trace the owners of their copyright but have not always been successful. My thanks are due to Olave, Lady Baden-Powell, to Lord Baden-Powell, and to Francis Baden-Powell, Esq., for permission to quote from the Founder's letters. The Headmaster of Charterhouse has agreed to my use of part of an article in *The Greyfriar*. The Scout Association has allowed reproduction of passages from *Scouting for Boys*, *Rovering to Success* and sundry papers. The Hamlyn Publishing Group have given permission to quote from *Lessons from the 'Varsity of Life*, *The Adventures of a Spy* and *An Old Wolf's Favourites*. To all of these, I express my sincere thanks and, if anyone has been omitted who should have been included, may I plead that it is in ignorance and not by intention.

The splendid portrait of Lord Baden-Powell on the jacket of the book is by David Jagger and is reproduced by kind permission of The Scout Association, as is also the original cover design of *Scouting for Boys* by John Hassall. All the other line drawings are by Lord Baden-Powell himself. It has been impossible to trace the owners of these which is the reason for the absence of any acknowledgment.

My thanks are also due to members of the Baden-Powell family and of The Scout Association for reading the manuscript and making suggestions. In particular, may I mention the assistance given by Rex Hazlewood, Esq., former General Editor of The Scout Association, and by Ron Jeffries, Esq., his successor.

MARY DREWERY

Foreword

HERE COMES A story of a great man who was also a happy man, in that he made the most of his opportunities to benefit himself and, whilst doing that, he gave happiness to others.

He has left, through the Scouts and Guides of the world, a call to shape their lives on that same pattern, and through these few lines I express the hope that as you read these pages you may gain strength and inspiration to follow his example.

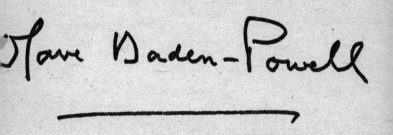

Mave Baden-Powell

Contents

Drawings

Maps

CHAPTER I

Man in the Making

THE BATTLE RAGED long and fierce. Broken bottles, stones, brick-ends and the refuse of the market were hurled over the high wall that divided the school from the waste land beyond, wrecking the football match that was in progress. Angry sixth-formers climbed out over the wall to drive off the attackers. Once again, the 'yobs' of Smithfield Market in the City of London were fighting the 'toffs' of Charterhouse — for that was how each side regarded the other.

Outside, the howls of derision from the enemy redoubled in intensity. It sounded as if the counter-attack was unsuccessful. To the sandy-haired, freckled youngster standing with a group of other first-year boys on the 'safe' side of the wall, the position was frustrating and humiliating. He was furious not to be able to join in for the honour of the school — but the top of the wall was beyond his reach and there was no ladder.

'If you went through that side door you could take them in the flank,' suggested a voice behind him.

He spun round in surprise to see the Headmaster.

'But we can't get out, sir,' said the boy. 'The door's locked.'

'How convenient that I have the key,' smiled Dr. Haig Brown, producing it from a pocket beneath his gown.

The first-formers needed no further prompting. They were out through the gate in a matter of seconds, yelling with defiance as they flung themselves into the fray. The Smithfield gang, surprised by the appearance of enemy reinforcements, turned to beat off the new threat. Upper school and first-formers pressed their attack from both sides. The enemy wavered, broke and finally fled in disorder. The honour of Charterhouse was saved and the thirteen-year-old schoolboy who was to become known all over the world as 'B.-P.' had his first lesson in military tactics.

It was all a very long time ago, in a different age. It is incredible to reflect that there were no lions in Trafalgar Square when B.-P. was born; they had not yet even been carved. Nor had the source of the River Nile been discovered, nor yet the motor car or the aeroplane been invented. The dust had scarcely settled on the reckless but glorious charge of the Light Brigade at Balaclava three years earlier. In America, it would be another four years before the first shots were fired in the Civil War. Only one third of Queen Victoria's long reign had passed for the year was 1857.

He did not start out as 'B.-P.' either, for the boy who was born on February 22nd, 1857 was christened Robert Stephenson Smyth Powell — 'Robert Stephenson' after his godfather (who was son of the George Stephenson who invented the 'Rocket' locomotive) and 'Smyth' after his mother's family. His father was a distinguished amateur astronomer, Fellow of the Royal Society, Savilian Professor of Geometry at Oxford and, like almost all university dons and school headmasters in those days, a clergyman. He died when 'Ste' or 'Stephe' (as B.-P. was known to the family) was only three years old. Out of respect for her husband, the young Mrs. Powell decided to incorporate her late husband's Christian name, Baden, into the family surname. Thus the future hero of Mafeking, the future founder of Scouting, became Robert Stephenson Smyth Baden-Powell.

B.-P.'s father married three times and B.-P. was the twelfth of his fourteen children. His mother, Henrietta Grace Smyth, was twenty-eight years younger than her brilliant husband. When he died in 1860, she was still only thirty-six — no age to have to cope with bringing up the seven children who had survived infancy and were still at home: Warington, George, Augustus, Frank, Stephe (B.-P.), Agnes and little Baden, only three weeks old. However, she was a woman of exceptional character and was determined that the children should not suffer in any way from the loss of their father.

She moved from the house in Stanhope Gardens, South Kensington, London, where B.-P. had been born, and bought Nos. 1 and 2 Hyde Park Gate. Here she entertained many of the giants of the day of literature, art and science. Robert Browning, the poet, was a frequent visitor and his son was a close friend of the older Powell boys. The eminent novelist, William Makepeace Thackeray, actually bribed B.-P. with a shilling to go back to bed when he had crept downstairs to peep at one of his mother's special dinner parties. Thomas Huxley, the biologist; Sir Joseph Hooker, the botanist; Dr. Jowett and Dean Stanley, both distinguished divines, were frequent visitors. John Ruskin, the art critic, was called in by a worried Mrs. Baden-Powell to advise on little Stephe's handling of pencils and paints. It seemed strange to her that he used either hand with equal facility.

'Let him draw as he will, madam,' advised Ruskin, so Stephe was allowed to develop the ambidextrous skill that enabled him in later life, as a parlour trick, to do two different drawings at the same time, one with either hand!

As would be expected of a clergyman's household, Stephe was brought up in an atmosphere where Christian principles were the accepted way of life. Though the pattern of worship might appear rigid and formal to today's Christians, the message of 'love your neighbour' got through to the young boy and stayed with him all his life.

During these middle years of Queen Victoria's reign, there was still a rigid class system, despite the rapid changes that were taking place in industry, science and exploration. The Victorian hymn, *All Things Bright and Beautiful*, used to contain a verse which today is no longer sung:

> The rich man in his castle,
> The poor man at his gate,
> God made them high and lowly
> And ordered their estate.

No-one in those days seemed to question whether or not those ideas were either correct or just and, indeed, little Stephe himself echoed them at the age of eight when he wrote *Laws for Me when I am Old:*

> I will have the poor people to be as rich as we are and all who go across the crossings shall give the poor crossing sweeper some money and you ought to thank God for what He has given us and He made the poor people to be poor and the rich people to be rich . . .

Probably compared with a crossing-sweeper, Mrs. Baden-Powell *was* rich but as Stephe grew up, he realised what a struggle his mother had had to spin out her limited resources to give her children the best possible opportunities in life. They themselves were early encouraged to be thrifty. Instead of individual pocket-money, there was a communal cash-box from which the family could draw according to their needs, but they had to leave in the box a note accounting for their withdrawals — an idea calculated to make each child careful not to be extravagant. Most of Stephe's early withdrawal notes read 'Orange — £0/0/1'.

He had a happy childhood. Many years later, in a letter to his future wife, he recalled the make-believe hours he spent with his brothers and sister in Kensington Gardens:

... You don't mean to say that YOU ever played by the Round Pond? That was MY playground. Oh I can show you where Red Indians lived and hunted. The Texan plains are within sight of it, where I've drawn an unerring bead on the wary bison (London sheep). The grizzly who lived under the chestnut trees towards the Albert Memorial — but why go on? If you never played there you never met them: if you did play there well of course you know all about it ...

Soon, however, Stephe was too old for such games, and too old for the school he attended in Kensington Square. If he was to attend public school like his older brothers (who had all been to St. Paul's) he would need to win a scholarship. He succeeded in this twice over — once for Fettes School in Edinburgh, the other for Charterhouse in the City of London. The latter would cost less in travelling so in 1870, at the age of thirteen, Stephe joined as a Gownboy Foundationer and met for the first time, in the clashes with the Smithfield boys, the reality of the class system he had so innocently accepted in *Laws for Me when I am Old*.

Two years later, the school moved from its restricted site in the City to the lovely open countryside near Godalming in Surrey where it stands today.

B.-P. was not an academic success. His school reports read:

Classics. Seems to me to take very little interest in his work.

Mathematics. Has to all intents given up the study of mathematics.

Science. Pays not the slightest attention, except in one week at the beginning of the quarter.

French. Could do well, but has become very lazy; often sleeps in school.

The Headmaster added at the bottom of the report: 'Your son's ability is greater than would appear by the results of the quarter. I am well satisfied with his conduct . . .'

Dr. Haig Brown was an exceptional headmaster. 'I am well satisfied with his conduct' revealed that he had discerned more in his reluctant pupil than his academic showing would indicate. The understanding of boys' nature that prompted him to hand over the key to the garden gate to allow Stephe and his friends to join in the Battle of Smithfield in 1870 also enabled him to recognise the talents that B.-P. was to put to such good use in later life. Moreover, Dr. Haig Brown was ahead of his time in appreciating that play-acting for young people is a useful means of education in that it not only trains the memory but gives a youngster assurance of manner and speech. B.-P. had natural acting ability and was constantly in demand for such parts as Cox in *Cox & Box* or Dogberry in *Much Ado*.

On one occasion he was sitting next to the headmaster at a school concert. Something went wrong behind the scenes and there was a pause in the proceedings that grew longer and longer. The audience began to fidget and cough.

'For goodness' sake, fill the gap,' muttered Haig Brown, whereat Stephe mounted the stage and, quite off the cuff, gave an hilarious impression of a French lesson. Had M. Buisson been present (and fortunately he was not) he would have been amazed at Stephe's mimicry of his accent for usually he dismissed his efforts to speak French with 'Badden Povvell' Hélas! It is in vain — it is not of use!'

Stephe was also an enthusiastic, if not brilliant footballer, usually playing in goal — which he guarded by the somewhat unorthodox tactic of letting out a blood-curdling yell just as an opposing player was about to shoot!

Inevitably, Baden-Powell was nicknamed 'Bathing-Towel' by his fellow pupils — a mispronunciation which caused him in later life to compose a helpful rhyme:

Man, matron, maiden,
Please call it Baden.
Further, for Powell,
Rhyme it with Noel.

On the whole, he was a bit of a 'loner' at school, somewhat reserved though never unpopular. He preferred the solitary pursuits of exploring the woods round Charterhouse. He wrote in *The Greyfriar* fifty years after the school had moved to Godalming:

> Why, man, it was only the other day — it can't be fifty years ago — that I was learning to snare rabbits in the copse at the 'new' Charterhouse, and to cook them, for secrecy, over the diminutive fire of a bushman. I learned, too, how to use an axe, how to walk across a gully on a felled tree-trunk, how to move silently through the bush so that one became a comrade rather than an interloper among the birds and animals that lived there. I knew how to hide my tracks, how to climb a tree and freeze up there while authorities passed below forgetting that they were *anthropoi* — being capable of looking up ...
>
> And the birds, the stoats, the watervoles that I watched and knew!
>
> These things stand out as if they were of yesterday. Cricket? Football? Athletics? Yes, I enjoyed them too; but they died long ago, they are only a memory, like much that I learnt at school. It was in the copse that I gained most of what helped me on in after life to find the joy of living.

The 'fagging' system at Charterhouse never worried B.-P. He was used to strict discipline in the family at home; indeed, fagging was positively restful compared with crewing for his oldest brother, Warington, who was twenty-three when Stephe started at Charterhouse. He was an enthusiast for any kind of sailing and Stephe's first water expedition was done with him the hard way, canoeing up the Thames to its source in Gloucestershire, then portaging the canoe overland to the Avon, from the Avon to the Severn and so to the Wye, eventually joining their mother and the younger children in Wales. Later, drawing on the family pool of resources, Warington designed and built first a 5-ton cutter, the *Diamond* and, two years later, a 10-tonner, the *Kohinoor*. The boats were berthed at Shanklin in the Isle of Wight but the Baden-Powell crew sailed far afield — round the north of Scotland, across to Norway, up and down the Channel coast. Warington was a strict captain and expected his crew of brothers, George, Frank and Stephe (Augustus had died of consumption at the age of thirteen) to jump to his orders with alacrity. The safety of the ship depended on their instant obedience and, indeed, this early experience of having to face danger and even death with equanimity was to be a splendid preparation for the many crises B.-P. had to face in later life.

They ran into danger on several occasions, not least one time when they followed the lifeboat out of Harwich harbour in response to a distress call. Warington had the laudable ambition of saving life — and was not unmindful that such a rescue might also bring a fortune in salvage money! The brothers sailed out into 'a hideous yellow tumbling sea' and thrashed around for hours without finding the ship in distress and losing sight of the lifeboat as well. They were overtaken by darkness and had a hard time of it beating back to Harwich, only to discover that the ship they had been seeking had been picked up by a tug and was safely in harbour.

Stephe, of course, as the youngest member of the crew was cabin-boy and, as such, responsible for cooking and washing-up. When he provided burnt stew, Warington as captain ordered the cook to 'eat the whole of this muck yourself' and commanded Frank to see that his order was enforced down to the last spoonful. No wonder the fagging system at Charterhouse held no problems for B.-P.!

Eventually he progressed to the sixth form and the great problem arose as to what he should do when he left school. The idea of taking up professionally either acting or drawing was dismissed out of hand. University must come first. Of course, everyone expected him to follow the family tradition and go to Oxford where his brother George had just won the Chancellor's prize. So in April 1876 B.-P. sat the entrance examination. Alas for his hopes! Dr. Jowett (despite being a family friend) rejected him as being 'not quite up to Balliol form'. Professor Dodgson of Christchurch (better known as Lewis Carroll, author of *Alice in Wonderland*) examined him in mathematics and discovered it was a subject about which B.-P. 'knew little or nothing'.

Dr. Haig Brown was disappointed; he had been sure that at least in interview B.-P.'s exceptional personality would have been recognised, despite his lack of academic ability. The Baden-Powell family were shocked. Whatever was to become of Stephe?

But Stephe, if he was disappointed, did not show it. His experiences sailing with Warington had taught him courage; and he had a natural resilience which, all his life, never let him be cast down for long. If one route was closed, there was always another way forward if one looked for it.

One morning shortly after his rejection by Oxford, he came upon an announcement of an Open Competitive Examination for commissions in Her Majesty's Army. There were to be a hundred appointments to infantry regiments, thirty commissions in the cavalry. B.-P. had not until then considered a career in the Army. There was no tradition of service life in his father's family; but his mother's father had been an admiral and her brother was a colonel. If they could make a success of a Service career, no doubt he could too. He was of the required age to enter for the examination and of the subjects demanded only his geometry was hopeless. So he set to and learnt by heart the seven books of Euclid's theorems required for the examination! From 3rd to 17th July, 1876, B.-P. sat the various papers along with 717 other 'gentlemen', as the Army authorities courteously described them. When the results were announced, B.-P. had been placed fifth for Infantry, second for Cavalry. As far as Euclid and Geometry were concerned, B.-P.'s cramming had paid off — though he readily admitted that the real meaning of the subject always remained a closed book to him.

Of course, an Army commission in the 1870s was not the well-paid profession it is today. Officers were expected to have private incomes to supplement their meagre pay. Expenses, particularly in a cavalry regiment, were high. However, a commission in the cavalry was considered far superior to one in the infantry so, as always in matters affecting the household, Mrs. Baden-Powell called a family council. Just as all had contributed in the past to the communal cash-box for pocket-money, now all still contributed to a communal fund for family expenses. The older brothers agreed that the fund should subsidise Stephe until he had established himself in his new career.

Successful officer candidates normally had to spend two years at Sandhurst Military Academy before being assigned to regiments but in those days the top six in the examination lists were excused this preliminary. On September 11th, 1876, B.-P. was gazetted a sub-lieutenant in the 13th Hussars and on October 30th he sailed from Portsmouth aboard the *Serapis* to join the regiment in India. He took with him two things from his Charterhouse days: the memory of Dr. Haig Brown's advice on tactics and a box containing the texts of all the plays he had appeared in while at school.

'It makes me almost think that he cannot have tried to do his best when he came up here,' Dr. Jowett wrote from Balliol when Mrs. Baden-Powell wrote to inform him of Stephe's success. 'I am sorry that he did not come again unless (as I dare to say) he likes his present place better than anything Oxford could offer him.'

It might be interesting to speculate how B.-P. might have developed if he *had* gone up to Oxford, though his life could scarcely have proved more exciting or far-reaching in its influence. 'If you are a square peg,' B.-P. said, 'keep your eye on a square hole and see that you get there.' His own square hole was the Army and his 'present place' was India where he landed on December 6th, 1876.

CHAPTER 2

Hussar in India

THE BRITISH HAD been in India as traders since the seventeenth century but only during the nineteenth century had they attempted to bring unity to the mixed races of that vast subcontinent. The advent of the railway and the telegraph hastened the process and a number of enlightened British administrators began to train the Indians themselves in the work of government. Sometimes the process of westernisation went too fast and offended the religious sensibilities of Hindu and Moslem alike. Such a factor had in 1857 triggered off the Indian Mutiny among native troops; but that uprising had been confined to the upper Ganges area while the rest of the country had remained loyal to the British administration. Now, almost twenty years later, Queen Victoria was to be proclaimed Empress of India at an Imperial Durbar in Delhi on January 1st, 1877.

This event was, indirectly, to give B.-P. his first test in command for after only two weeks in Lucknow, the senior officers left to represent the regiment at the Durbar and Sub-Lieutenant Baden-Powell remained behind in solitary command of Troop B, 13th Hussars.

The very first morning, he had the men paraded in two ranks for inspection. He had been particularly instructed by his C.O. to check that each of the men was wearing his 'cholera belt', it being the mistaken belief a hundred years ago that the wearing of a heavy band of flannel round the waist would ward off that dreadful disease. The cholera belt was hot and uncomfortable and the men hated it.

As B.-P. turned at the end of the front rank of troops, he noticed out of the corner of his eye a man from the rear rank

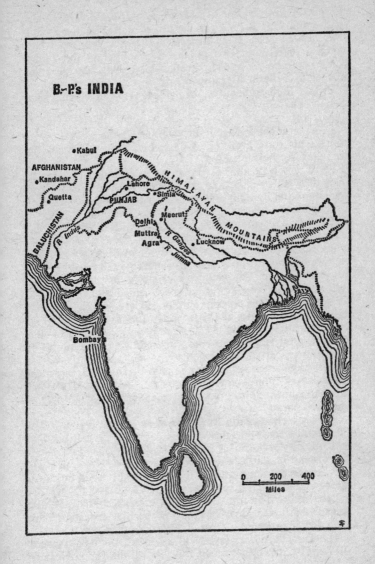

B.-P.'s INDIA

Kabul
AFGHANISTAN
Kandahar
Quetta
BALUCHISTAN
Lahore
PUNJAB
Simla
Delhi
Meerut
Muttra
Agra
Lucknow
R. Indus
R. Ganges
R. Jumna
HIMALAYAN MOUNTAINS
Bombay

0   200   400
Miles

slip quickly into the line already inspected. Why? The young subaltern walked slowly along the rear file debating in his mind what line to take. It so happened that the man who had switched places was, in fact, the only soldier in the Troop whose name he yet knew! Trusting his hunch, he called the man out to the front after inspection.

'Private Ramsbotham,' he demanded. 'Are you wearing your cholera belt?'

'No, sir.'

'Don't let it happen again, Private Ramsbotham.' B.-P. tried to make his voice gruff and experienced. 'You will wear two belts until further notice.'

The Troop were impressed that the young officer apparently knew them all by name and the luckless Private Ramsbotham was relieved to have his offence dealt with promptly instead of being put on a charge. This is the first recorded instance of B.-P.'s fair and commonsense attitude towards discipline.

He had been disappointed that almost the first question asked of him by his Adjutant on arriving in Lucknow had had nothing to do with his riding or shooting ability but the un-military question 'Can you act — or sing — or paint scenery?' He could in fact do all three but they seemed strange talents to commend him to his superior officers. He was soon to learn that the two chief enemies of the troops in India were disease and boredom. Cholera could kill; dysentery and fever could pull a man down physically; but boredom could wreck his morale or send him out at risk to seek his entertainment in the native bazaars. Thus each regiment tried to put on as much theatrical and musical entertainment as possible. B.-P. could scarcely have brought with him a more valuable item of luggage than his boxful of plays.

But regimental life in India was expensive for a young sub-altern whose only income was his pay. B.-P.'s half-brother, Baden Henry (who was a Judge in the Punjab) used occasion-ally to send him a little extra but there was never enough. He was determined not to call on the communal fund at home for more money so he scrimped and saved on his mess bills in order to live within his income. He gave up smoking, drank very little and spent as much time as possible in the mess instead of in his bungalow in order to cut down the cost of native servants.

However, the money saved still would not run to polo ponies. B.-P. was a daring horseman and, like all the young Hussars, was keen to join the polo-playing set of the regiment — but polo was a dangerous sport and inexperienced players were not allowed to practise on the regimental ponies. Moreover, the pace of the game was such that several ponies were required by each player. Trained animals would be way beyond B.-P.'s means so he decided the only way to acquire his own string was to buy the ponies cheap and train them himself.

His first purchase was from a man who made his living cutting grass and selling it as horse fodder. 'Hercules' was a miserably thin chestnut who earned his name because he used to carry for his owner huge loads of grass almost as big as himself. B.-P. and Hercules learned to play polo together.

While I learned to hit the ball as we galloped along, Hercules learned that it was his business to take me wherever the ball was going as fast as he possibly could. He got to be quite quick at seeing the ball and trying to follow it. Very often his sharp eyes would find it through a cloud of dust before I saw it for myself, and away he would go carrying me to it.

Eventually, through prudent buying and training and trading of horses, B.-P. built up for himself a string of seven excellent ponies.

Life was not all polo and play-acting. His first eight months in Lucknow were 'garrison training' which involved 'a continued round of drill and duty from morn to dewy eve' — riding school, garrison class, sword exercises, cavalry instruction, carbine practice, elementary drill. At the end of July 1877, he passed his first examination and was put on to yet another course to fit him for promotion. So far, however, he had done nothing in the army except train. That summer he hoped to escape to do a real job of work. There was severe famine in southern India and army officers were called upon to assist with relief work. B.-P. immediately and eagerly volunteered but, to his great chagrin, was turned down because his Hindustani was not sufficiently fluent. It seemed that even in the army he was not to escape 'swotting' — and he might not even have started on learning Hindustani had it not been for a chance encounter the previous February.

After one of the regimental theatrical performances, B.-P. had been invited with the other officers to a ball. He went to the buffet to fetch ices for his partner and himself but had great difficulty in making his wants understood by the Indian waiter. A short but soldierly man standing beside him translated his order into fluent Hindustani, then turned to B.-P. and said: 'Young fellow, you will make your life happier here if you learn a bit of the language. Who are you and where are you staying?'

B.-P. gave him the details, collected the two ices and promptly forgot about the encounter. However, the next day there arrived at his bungalow a native teacher of languages who announced that he had been sent to B.-P. by General Sir Frederick Roberts!

But the young officer was 'burning the candle at both ends' — not a wise thing to do in the climate of India. He was working all day at his military duties, playing hard at polo and theatricals when off duty, and working far into the small hours swotting up military law and administration for his next examination. He had a sharp bout of fever when he was due to sit his papers and felt so ill that he was quite convinced he had failed. However, to his surprise and delight he passed First Class with a 'star' or distinction in surveying and was promptly promoted to full lieutenant.

A short leave in the Himalayan mountain resort of Simla did little to restore his health. On his return to the intense heat of Lucknow, he went down again with repeated headaches, attacks of fever and steady loss of weight. By November he was in hospital and was in such a feeble state that he was shipped home to England on sick leave, sailing from Bombay two years to the day from when he first landed there.

He returned to a different home in London, for during his absence abroad, his mother had moved to a bigger and finer house, 8 St. George's Place, Hyde Park Corner. Mrs. Baden-Powell was thrilled to have all her family together under one roof and would probably have liked to have kept it that way for ever. She did not like the idea of any of her children marrying. She wanted the 'communal chest' to continue all through their lives and dismissed the idea of a son's marriage as 'the selfish ordinary life of earning and spending for himself alone.'

The sea journey home to England and two months' loving care on the part of his mother and sister Agnes completely restored B.-P. to health. He was thrilled to be able to attend real theatres again and delighted in the latest Gilbert & Sullivan operas, *H.M.S. Pinafore* and *The Pirates of Penzance*. He went on a musketry and signalling course at Hythe in Kent but later felt frustrated that he was 'trapped' there for months on end instead of being back in India with his regiment — for it looked as if they would be in action before long.

There had been trouble on the north-west frontier on and off for the past forty years. Britain was anxious lest Afghanistan, which formed a buffer between Russia and India, would ally itself with Russia whose massed forces threatened the Indian border. There had been constant inter-tribal wars and massacres but now, in 1880, a number of dissident chiefs under Ayub Khan had proclaimed a 'jehad' or holy war against the British 'infidels'. The two armies clashed at Maiwand on July 27th. The British forces were hopelessly outnumbered. Half were killed outright; the remainder struggled back to Kandahar, many dying of thirst and exhaustion on the way. The situation was disastrous. The remnants of the British expedition were besieged in Kandahar by the exultant forces of Ayub Khan who had merely to wait until the garrison was weak enough to be taken by storm.

When the news reached England, public opinion was horrified. The defeat must be avenged. On August 11th, General Roberts (the same one who had advised B.-P. to learn Hindustani) set out from Kabul, the Afghan capital, with a force of 10,000 men. There were 313 miles of wild mountain and barren desert to cross before he could reach Kandahar. Roberts and his men made it in twenty days' march. On September 1st, he flung his army, all 'in famous health and spirits' despite their arduous and desperate march, against Ayub Khan's besieging army. The Afghans were completely routed; Ayub Khan fled; and that was how General Roberts came to receive the title of 'Lord Roberts of Kandahar'.

But if the immediate war in Afghanistan seemed to be over, there were still rumblings of rebellion. The 13th Hussars would be sure to be sent up to the Frontier. B.-P. fretted through his musketry course and the remainder of the summer. But he managed to pass First Class and by October 3rd 1880 was once again aboard the *Serapis* on his way back to India.

He found that the regiment was already in Kandahar and made haste to join them there. The city bore evidence of the bitter siege. The walls were pitted with shot and the ramparts were still piled with sandbags.

Just as at Charterhouse, B.-P. had been fortunate in having an unconventional headmaster in Dr. Haig Brown, so in the

13th Hussars he was equally fortunate in having an unconventional commanding officer. Colonel Baker Russell, unlike the usual officer of that period, did not go by the strict letter of *Queen's Regulations* but preferred to use his initiative. He looked for imagination in his officers and must have recognised the potential of young Baden-Powell. He remembered his 'star' for surveying in the examinations at Lucknow so gave him the assignment of surveying the battlefield at Maiwand to see what evidence he could collect to account for the British defeat there five months earlier. It was a grisly business. 'Any amount of dead horses,' he wrote home, 'lines of cartridge cases, wheel tracks and hoof marks quite clear, dead men in heaps — most had been hurriedly buried, and dug up again by jackals — clothes and accoutrements all over the place.'

This incident had two important results. It brought home to the young officer the grim realities of war; although he was to make a brilliant career in the Army in the future, his aim was always to defeat the enemy by outwitting rather than by killing him. The other result was that the detailed maps B.-P. prepared of the site of the Maiwand battle and which were used in the ensuing court proceedings brought him to the notice of Sir Garnet Wolseley, later to become Commander-in-Chief of the British Army.

B.-P. did not see any action on this tour of duty although he gained much military experience leading mounted patrols to discourage any further attacks by hostile tribesmen. Inevitably, in such an out-of-the-way outpost, he was asked by Col. Baker Russell to arrange entertainment for the troops.

During the interval of one such concert, there was a stir at the back of the hall. Men began to jump to attention as a thin grey-haired general made his way down the aisle to the front.

'At ease, men, at ease,' he said kindly as the young officers and troops sprang to attention on seeing him. Col. Baker Russell was full of apologies. 'We hadn't expected you, sir.' He offered the general a seat in the front row.

'No, thank you,' replied the general. 'I've come to talk to the men.'

With these words, the visiting general mounted the stage and broke into song:

'I am the very model of a modern Major-General.
I've information vegetable, animal and mineral.

I know the Kings of England
And I quote the fights historical
From Marathon to Waterloo, in order categorical ...'

Of course, it was B.-P. — singing one of the numbers from
the new Gilbert & Sullivan opera he had seen while on leave,
The Pirates of Penzance! Luckily he knew his C.O. to be a
good sport, otherwise he might well have found himself on a
charge — he always had an irrepressible sense of mischief.

Afterwards, the regiment staged the whole opera, but, as
there was no hall in Kandahar big enough to accommodate the
large cast, rehearsals and performances were held out of doors,
with the stage marked out by swords stuck in the ground so that
the cast would have their weapons ready to hand if attacked by
tribesmen.

When the Afghanistan troubles had quietened down, the
regiment was posted to Quetta in Baluchistan where they remained for six months. Here B.-P. began further to develop
those special abilities in scouting and stalking that he had practised in the woods around Charterhouse. During a night exercise, he penetrated right into the middle of the 'enemy' camp
and made a note of the various dispositions of the forces. Before
retiring in the same stealthy way in which he had come, he took
the precaution of leaving one of his gloves under a bush from
where he had made his observations. At the end of the exercise,
the officers from both sides were called in to give their reports.
B.-P. staggered the judges by giving a detailed and exact report
on the enemy positions. The 'enemy' hotly refuted the suggestion that he could have obtained this information by reconnaissance; it must just be an inspired guess, they said.
However, they had to change their tune when B.-P. led them to
the bush and showed his glove marking the point to which he
had penetrated.

In Quetta also, he started on another means of raising
money. It was to bring in useful additional revenue over the
years. He had always had a talent for drawing and had illustrated his letters home with amusing sketches round the edge of
the paper. His caricatures of brother officers had also been
eagerly sought after. Now he put this talent to commercial use
by sending back to England illustrated articles for the newspapers. There were no cheap photographic illustrations in
newspapers in the 1880s and, of course, no filmed or television

reporting, so the public welcomed 'on the spot' drawings of the unfamiliar, faraway places that came into the news.

By Christmas of 1881, the 13th were back in India and stationed at Muttra on the river Jumna. B.-P. shared a nine-roomed bungalow with another officer, Lieut. Kenneth McLaren, always known as 'The Boy' because he only looked about fourteen. Between them, they built up a good stable for they were both keen polo players and, with Lieut. MacDougall and Capt. Braithwaite, made an almost unbeatable team that carried off the honours for the 13th in most of the inter-regimental polo matches at Agra and Meerut.

B.-P. spent three busy and enjoyable years in Muttra. He became Adjutant to Col. Baker Russell and was promoted captain at the age of twenty-six. He was musketry instructor, riding master, directed the regimental theatre and managed the band. In addition — and this was to prove one of his most important activities — he ran classes for N.C.O.s giving instruction in reconnaissance and scouting.

Pig-sticking

Early in January, 1882, he had been introduced to the 'sport of rajahs' — pig-sticking. This was a skilled and dangerous sport which consisted of hunting on horse-back the native wild boar — a large, fast animal reputedly the most savage in the world and one which could cause untold havoc to crops in cultivated areas. The aim was to ride down the boar with a lance. The chase required every ounce of skill the horseman could muster for the boar was cunning and knew how to twist and turn, using all available cover. Soon B.-P. was training horses for pig-sticking as well as for polo and indeed, won the Kadir Cup with Patience, one of his two best horses. In a letter home, he gives an amusing account of his adventures on the other horse, Hagarene:

> Such excitement! ... Away goes a great pig. 'Ride!' — and away we go. Hagarene soon gets away from the rest — the pig dashes into thick grass jungle — but I am pretty close to him and can just see him every now and then. Great tussocks of grass six feet high. Haggy bounding through them — then twenty yards of open ground, then into a fresh patch of jungle thicker than the others. Suddenly a bright green sort of hedge appears in front. As the pig disappears through it, Haggy leaps it and there, eight feet below it, is a placid pond — the pig goes plump under the water and Haggy and self ditto almost on top of him — right down we go to any depth — a deal of struggling — striking out — hanging on to weeds, etc. And I emerge on the far bank — and see Haggy climbing out too — and away she goes for camp — and the pig I can see skulking away in some weeds ...

One would have thought that B.-P. would have been satisfied with his success in the Kadir Cup, with his polo, his interesting work and his popularity as an actor. Not so. Mrs. Baden-Powell had imbued into her boys a deep spirit of competition and B.-P. was beginning to realise that his brothers were more successful than he was. Baden Henry, his half-brother, had published five books on India. Warington, the stern 'captain' of his boyhood trips to sea, had written a book on canoeing. George, who was making a career in the Colonial Office, had had three books published. Frank was making a name for himself as a marine painter. Even Baden, the 'baby' of the family, was becoming well known for his experiments with man-carrying kites and military ballooning. Yet so far, all B.-P. had achieved in print were a few articles and drawings in *The Graphic*.

On his brother George's advice, B.-P. polished up the lectures he had been giving to his N.C.O.s and sent them off to a publisher in England. Perhaps they might bring him to the notice of some high official in the Army; if a young officer wished to advance his career in peacetime, he had in some way to draw attention to any particular skills he might have. These lecture notes were eventually published in book form in 1884 under the title *Reconnaissance & Scouting*. He also began to write a book on pig-sticking but before he could finish it, he had been whirled into an altogether different kind of life.

In the autumn of 1883, Queen Victoria's third son, Prince Arthur, Duke of Connaught, came out to India with his wife to take up at Meerut the appointment of Divisional-General. Inevitably, in the closed community of a garrison town, B.-P. came to the Duke's notice in various ways — through his acting, through the band and so on. But the big moment came on his 27th birthday, February 22nd, 1884, when, as the winner of the Kadir Cup, he was asked to initiate the Duke into the mysteries of the sport of pig-sticking.

They had a splendid run and the Duke was first up to the pig and secured the honour of 'first spear' and this was the beginning of a firm friendship that lasted for over fifty years. Shortly afterwards, B.-P. was assigned to the Duke as aide-de-camp and found himself caught up in a glamorous social life that set his mother at home worrying lest some young woman would lure him away from her closely-knit family circle.

'Don't feel nervous, Ma,' her son wrote to her. '. . . I'm going to wait until I'm a major and then it will be a £50,000 girl at home.'

It looked as if he might well be able to begin looking for such a girl for in November, 1884 the 13th Hussars completed their tour of duty in India. As the train jogged halfway across the continent to Bombay, B.-P. was able to realise at least one of his ambitions: as his godfather's father had invented the first locomotive, it seemed all wrong for him never to have driven one. 'So I got on terms with the driver and took my place on the footplate,' he wrote in *Indian Memories* 'and was very soon, in my own estimation, quite a capable driver.'

But the *Serapis,* once again carrying the 13th Hussars out of Bombay, did not sail for England. At the last moment, the regiment was ordered to Durban. There was trouble with the Boers in South Africa.

CHAPTER 3

The Amateur Spy

UNLIKE INDIA WHERE British rule extended from the Himalayas to the southern tip of Ceylon, Africa up to the 1880s had not been colonised by the British. Their only concern with the 'dark continent' had been to create small coastal settlements in the interests of trade and also to provide safe ports for squadrons of the navy. To put it simply, British interest in Africa was largely to protect trade routes to and from India and the Far East. The opening of the Suez Canal in 1869 shifted Britain's sphere of interest to Egypt. For the rest, there were palm oil traders on the west coast, missionaries and explorers on the east.

By far and away the largest colonised area was in the south where the Boers — farmers of Dutch extraction — had been attracted by the temperate climate. But in 1805 Britain annexed the Cape Colony to secure 'the master link of connection between the western and eastern world' and during the years that followed, the Boers in the Cape Colony became restless under the British administration. In particular, they did not like the British policy of protecting the interests of the native population so they trekked north to settle in the area around the River Vaal, establishing the Transvaal (north of the river) in 1852 and the Orange Free State (south of the river) in 1854. Britain, not wanting to lose control of the coast, promptly annexed the province of Natal which lay between the two Boer states and the sea.

The new states soon ran into trouble. If the Boers had felt they had to escape from what they regarded as 'British tyranny', they found themselves in even deeper trouble from the attacks of savage Matabele to the north, Basutos to the south and Zulus on their south-eastern border. Moreover, the Boers were quarrelling among themselves over political and religious

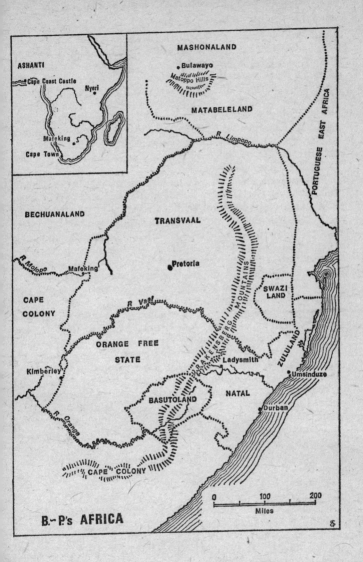

ASHANTI

Cape Coast Castle

Nyeri

Mafeking

Cape Town

MASHONALAND

• Bulawayo

Matoppo Hills

MATABELELAND

R. Limpopo

PORTUGUESE EAST AFRICA

BECHUANALAND

TRANSVAAL

R Molopo

Mafeking

• Pretoria

DRAKENSBERG MOUNTAINS

SWAZI LAND

CAPE COLONY

R Vaal

ORANGE FREE STATE

ZULULAND

Kimberley

Ladysmith

• Umsinduze

R Orange

BASUTOLAND

NATAL

• Durban

CAPE COLONY

0   100   200
Miles

B.-P.'s AFRICA

questions. By 1877 the affairs of the Transvaal were in such hopeless confusion that the British Government decided to annexe the province to save it from economic collapse. So now Britain took on new burdens not only in the form of a resentful Boer population but also in the form of a series of small wars against the various African tribes who threatened the boundaries of the Transvaal. In 1879 there was bitter fighting against the Zulus led by Chief Cetywayo, which was only settled after dreadful slaughter on both sides. Then the Transvaal Boers rose in revolt and, after inflicting several humiliating defeats on the British forces, once again secured self-government for themselves. The year was 1881.

Now it was the Boers' turn to expand and they began to encroach into Bechuanaland and into the northern part of Cape Province around Mafeking. Repeated warnings had no effect so by 1884 it was decided that a show of force was necessary. General Sir Charles Warren was sent into Bechuanaland with a force of 4,000 men (including B.-P.'s brother George as political adviser) to secure the border with the Transvaal. It was this crisis which brought the 13th Hussars to Africa. They were to be held in readiness in Natal in case a diversionary attack was needed on the other side of the Transvaal.

In the event, nothing happened. The dispute was settled without fighting and the 13th Hussars resumed their regular routine of drill and lectures. No pig-sticking; there were no pigs. No polo; the fields were too hilly and broken. Moreover, the officers had had to leave their ponies behind in India. How B.-P. wished he could be with his younger brother, Baden, who was with the Camel Corps in Egypt fighting another 'holy war' stirred up by the fanatical Mahdi! He occupied his spare time working on his book on pig-sticking and expanding his lecture notes on cavalry training for possible publication as a manual of cavalry instruction.

Although the crisis over Bechuanaland seemed to have simmered down, the 13th's C.O., Colonel Baker Russell, was taking no chances. If he had to move his men swiftly from Natal into the Transvaal and the Orange Free State, he wanted to know all the possible routes through the Drakensberg Mountains that defended the border. His maps were incomplete and although he knew that the two main passes were in Boer hands, he felt sure that there must be others which could be used. B.P. was sent off alone to make a secret reconnaissance.

It was an assignment exactly suited to his taste and to his varied talents. He grew a scraggy beard, put on shabby civilian clothes and disappeared into the mountains with two horses, one for riding, the other for carrying his blankets and rations. It was difficult terrain to traverse. The Drakensbergs were harsh, bare mountains, flat-topped but ridged with sheer, precipitous slopes. He was away for three weeks, covering hundreds of miles on horseback, sometimes sleeping rough under the stars, sometimes putting up for the night at Boer farms on the pretence that he was prospecting the area 'with a view to recommending the country for immigration'. He learned to respect and admire the hard-working Boer farmers, though he found it difficult to get on friendly terms with them for they were a dour people. No-one suspected his true identity and, indeed, so good was his disguise that he was not even recognised by one of his own officers. 'Get out!' the Major growled savagely when an apparently ruffianly stranger greeted him by name!

While surveying and sketching the territory, B.-P. discovered that the maps he had been given were not only incomplete but inaccurate in many particulars. He made the necessary corrections and also studied the terrain from a strategic angle. On his return, he submitted several tactical recommendations. As matters turned out, B.-P.'s survey proved not after all to be needed so his maps were filed away somewhere and forgotten. With the benefit of hindsight, it can be seen that *had* his suggestions been heeded, Sir George White's division need not have been holed up for four months in Ladysmith fourteen years later when the Boer War was fought. *Had* his corrections been transferred to any new maps issued, Sir Redvers Buller need not have been defeated at the Battle of Colenso — for the map he used showed a mountain on the wrong side of the Tugela River!

More important for the future was that the assignment enabled B.-P. to use all the skills of observation, drawing, acting and so on that he had been developing since childhood. It gave him a taste for the 'flannel-shirt life' he was later to introduce to boys of all classes and creeds and nations, and it laid the foundation of his love of Africa. This time, however, his visit to the continent was to be a short one. There was just time for a two-month safari in Portuguese East Africa before the 13th Hussars were ordered back to England. Guy Fawkes Day, 1885, saw them newly quartered at Norwich.

Two years in England enabled B.-P. to try out several innovations that his service to date had suggested. Though still a
young officer, he was none-the-less critical that the army clung
to outdated methods because they were 'in the book'. For
example, he introduced the use of hand signals instead of
shouted orders. This is a commonplace of army tactics today
but in the last century, as he had observed on the north-west
frontier, noisy British patrols advertised their presence to every
tribesman for miles around.

He also during this period embarked on his career as a spy.
'Espionage' has to some extent become a dirty word in the
modern age but, as B.-P. was at pains to point out, spying is the
peacetime equivalent of what is called 'reconnaissance' or
'scouting' in time of war. It requires the same courage and
resourcefulness but the penalties for failure are much more
harsh. The only time spying was to be condemned, he maintained, was when the spy was acting as a traitor to his own
country.

In these days of microfilm, bugging devices and surveillance
by satellite, B.-P.'s methods may appear almost naïve but they
were perfectly adequate for the age in which he lived — and
possibly required even more personal courage and ingenuity
than today's sophisticated operations.

It seems incredible that smokeless powder was not invented
until 1884. It created a revolution in the design of firearms.
The new propellant was much more reliable than the old black
powder and it was now possible to produce guns that re-loaded
automatically. B.-P. followed these developments with interest.
He visited Armstrong's works where the latest machine-guns
were being manufactured and mastered all the details of the
British weapon. At the same time, however, the German High
Command announced a new machine-gun. They had made
available in the press announcements certain details about its
calibre but its speed of firing and its reliability were still
closely guarded secrets. Germany and Russia were also experimenting with new types of military balloons and Russia had
developed a powerful searchlight.

B.-P. and his brother Baden (now an officer in the Scots
Guards) decided — very recklessly and quite unofficially — to
see what they could discover about these new developments.
They were fortunate enough to have their leave coincide in
1886 so decided to go to Berlin. They managed to pick up the

information they wanted about the machine-gun at Spandau without attracting attention to themselves and, flushed with success, moved on to the Russian manoeuvres at Krasnoe Selo.

B.-P. had early realised that wigs and false moustaches were all right for stage disguise but not in real life. As he had established in Natal the previous year, the safest disguise was to look as if one had good reason to be in the area. Thus, at Krasnoe Selo, he and Baden put up at a local inn near the station and spent their days as any two holiday-makers might, on long walking expeditions — except that their walks took them round the perimeter of the area where the balloon and searchlight experiments were taking place.

The area was ringed with notice-boards forbidding entry. The brothers decided that boldness was their best course. If it was prohibited to *enter* the area, then they could be fairly confident that, once they were safely inside, everyone they met would assume that they had a right to be there. So, having found a way past the guards, they walked around boldly, saluting everyone that anybody else saluted and generally wearing an air of confidence they were far from feeling. They even managed to examine the gondola of the new balloon during a luncheon-break for the Russians were so confident of their security that they did not leave a guard on it. The brothers stayed on in the test area until the evening so that they could watch the new searchlight in operation, then slipped quietly back to their inn without being discovered.

But it is possible to ride one's luck too hard. They learned that Czar Alexander III was to attend the last night of the manoeuvres and guessed that every latest device would be displayed for his benefit. They arranged, therefore, that Baden would observe from a point outside the area of the manoeuvres while B.-P. would sneak back to their previous position inside the perimeter. When he arrived, he found the place so overrun with security guards on account of the Czar's visit that he decided it would be too risky to stay. Unfortunately, as he walked back along the road in the dark towards his rendezvous with Baden, he was caught in the light of the lamps of the first carriage of the Czar's entourage. He should have brazened things out and saluted smartly and would probably not have been discovered. On this occasion he seems unfortunately not to have been his usual alert self for he made the mistake of turning his face away from the light. This drew attention to him and he was promptly arrested.

He tried to talk his way out of the situation by explaining that he was an Englishman on holiday who had lost his way and please could they direct him to the station? But the story was unconvincing; why should an English tourist be abroad in that particular area in darkness? Fortunately, there was nothing to connect B.-P. with the army or things might have gone much worse for him. As it was, his passport was removed and he was placed under 'open arrest' in an hotel in St. Petersburg (now Leningrad).

His position was precarious; the penalty for spying could be as much as five years' imprisonment without trial. His every movement was watched by a plain-clothes detective in the hotel and B.-P. knew that whatever he did was reported to the authorities. Recovering his poise, he decided to use the Russians' very vigilance to effect his escape. He announced one morning (within hearing of the detective) that he was fed up with being under open arrest, that he was not going to put up with it any longer, that he was going to take the next train to Berlin and from there return to England. With this, he ostentatiously hailed a cab and directed that he be driven to the station. He guessed that the detective would immediately report his words and that a reception committee would await him at the station barrier. However, he had no intention of going to the station. No sooner had the cab turned the corner than he told the driver to take him to the docks. There he found a ship sailing for Denmark on the next tide and persuaded the captain to give him a passage.

Back safely in England, he rejoined his detachment and went up to Seaforth near Liverpool in May of 1887 where he became involved in the preparations for a grand Military Tournament to celebrate Queen Victoria's Golden Jubilee. One item in which he and his men took part was a mock reconnaissance by cavalry in enemy country. The scene ended with a dramatic cavalry charge across the arena in which the 'foe' was completely routed. To give the scene in the Tournament greater reality, he persuaded the inventor of the new Nordenfelt machine-gun to lend him one and to mount it on a 'galloping carriage'.

A day or two later, his sergant hurried into his quarters to tell him that the Adjutant-General of the British Army was below and wanted to see him. B.-P. smiled as he descended unhurriedly to the square. Adjutant-Generals do not call on mere captains; they send for them. It was the fashion at that time with everyone from the Prince of Wales downwards to carry out elaborate practical jokes. Who was staging a leg-pull this time? But he snapped to attention when he saw that it was indeed Lord Wolseley in the square.

Wolseley had heard of the Hussars' item in the Tournament and had been particularly interested in the new machine-gun and its 'galloping carriage'. Would it be possible to use it with cavalry in rough country? They decided to have a trial run and, with Wolseley sitting on the gun and B.-P. on one of the horses, they did 'a real up-and-down switchback performance' over the sand-dunes. The trial must have been satisfactory for the Nordenfelt machine-gun was adopted officially for the British cavalry and B.-P. was seconded to Aldershot to instruct officers in its use. He also invented and patented a quick release harness for detaching the gun from the horse-team towing it.

Then came an opportunity for him to return to Africa. His uncle, General Henry A. Smyth, had been appointed G.O.C. South Africa. Would Stephe care to be his aide-de-camp? It meant leaving the regiment. It meant giving up practical soldiering for a glamorous but less challenging job — but it did mean a return to Africa and that was enough for B.-P. He had lost his heart to the 'dark continent' and by the end of 1887 he was on his way back to it.

CHAPTER 4

Dinuzulu's Necklace

IF HE HAD hoped by returning to Africa that he might resume the 'flannel-shirt life' that had so attracted him in Natal, B.-P. was to be sadly disappointed. The work, he complained in a disillusioned letter home, was like having a rest-cure 'which, at my time of life, seems hardly necessary'. His uncle the General was kind and sought to teach his impetuous nephew prudence but, even combining with his responsibilities as A.D.C. the duties of Acting Military Secretary, B.-P.'s position was really an office job.

There went with his duties, of course, a rich and varied social life in which his Aunt Connie, the general's wife, encouraged her nephew to take part. Many a thirty-year-old would have revelled in a round of balls, race-meetings, hunting, theatricals and dinner parties that brought him into the Government House circle but B.-P. was ambitious for more than social climbing. He quickly found himself longing for some challenge to his military skill, some enterprise in which he could escape from the debilitating atmosphere of the Government House social round. It was not to his taste to be cross-examined by the Governor's wife, Lady Robinson, as to his preferences among the young ladies of the Cape or to have to give impromptu performances in front of the butler of whatever item he was to perform in the next concert, just because that formidable lady commanded him to do so! Relief from this artificial existence came with a sudden appeal for help from the Governor of Natal and Zululand.

After Sir Garnet Wolseley had defeated Cetywayo at Ulundi in 1879, that chieftain's kingdom had been broken up into several provinces, each under a Zulu chieftain (with the exception of one province which had a white 'chief' — John Dunn, a

Scottish trader who had spent a lifetime among the Zulus).
Inevitably, the small provinces started fighting among themselves and, with Boer assistance, Dinuzulu (son of Cetywayo)
emerged supreme. But the Boers demanded a price for their
help: the whole of the northern half of Zululand and a strip of
the country down the east coast. This was to provide them with
access to the sea and enough territory to found the New Repub-
lic of Vrijheid. Dinuzulu appealed to Britain for help but it was
too late to retrieve the land the Boers had already taken. In
order to prevent them taking more, Britain now annexed what
remained of Zululand. Although most of the Zulu chieftains
accepted British domination provided they were left in peace,
Dinuzulu bitterly resented Britain's action. With an army of
4,000 Usutu behind him, he openly defied British authority.
This encouraged other Zulu tribes to revolt and soon mission
stations were being attacked, stores looted and Europeans
massacred. The beginning of June 1888 found the resident
magistrate of Zululand besieged in the small fort of Umsinduze
along with 200 Europeans and 300 loyal natives.

It was at this point that the Governor felt events had moved
beyond his control and sent to the Cape for military assistance.
General Smyth immediately left for Durban with a force of
2,000 men, and B.-P. as one of his officers. On reaching Natal,
he detached a force of 400 cavalry to relieve Umsinduze; B.-P.
was on the Staff. On the second day of their march northwards
from Durban, they were joined by John Dunn and his *impi* of
2,000 loyal Zulus. B.-P. never forgot that first sight of Zulu
warriors. Years later he described the scene:

Shortly afterwards, I heard a sound in the distance which
at first I thought was an organ playing in Church, and I
thought for the moment that we must be approaching a
mission station over the brow of the hill. But when we topped
the rise we saw moving up towards us from the valley below
three long lines of men marching in single file and singing a
wonderful anthem as they marched . . .

The men themselves looked so splendid. They were . . .
fine, strong muscular fellows with handsome faces of a rich
bronze colour . . . They wore little in the way of clothing and
their brown bodies were polished with oil and looked like
bronze statues. Their heads were covered with ostrich
plumes and they had swaying kilts of foxes' tails . . . while

An Usutu warrior

round their knees and elbows were fastened white cows' tails as a sign they were on the warpath . . .

The combined force relieved Umsinduze where B.-P. found himself called upon to act as medical officer as well as staff officer. Then he was detailed to ascertain Dinuzulu's whereabouts and the strength of his army.

He organised a small group of Zulu scouts and set out to reconnoitre the area. Sometimes they came upon groups of Usutu separated from the main force but could find no trace of the rebel chief and his main army. On one expedition, however, B.-P. and his Zulu orderly were in advance of their party and came to the edge of a high cliff thickly overgrown with bushes. He was peering down into the valley below when his orderly yelled a warning. He spun round to face an Usutu warrior in full war-dress. The Usutu turned and fled, scrambling and stumbling down the cliff face. It would have been easy to shoot him but B.-P. wanted to know where he had been heading before he stumbled upon them.

B.-P. and his orderly followed along the scarcely recognisable track. Way below them, the Usutu suddenly disappeared from sight into what appeared to be a cave. They followed, but the opening proved not to be a cave, but a cleft in the rock-face which brought them out at the head of a parallel and deeper valley. Far below them on the floor of the valley they could see encamped a vast army of Usutu. So this was Dinuzulu's secret hiding place! Immediately below them, however, huddled in the gully beneath the 'back entrance' through which B.-P. had found his way into the hidden valley were hundreds of women and children. It was difficult at first to realise who or what they were for all he could see was a dark moving mass flecked with the whites of hundreds of rolling eyeballs!

B.-P. called on his orderly to address them in their own language and to tell them to surrender but it was no good; they were far too terrified to listen. B.-P. jumped down from the rock and began to move among them. At this they began to scream and cower away from him, convinced that the killing was about to begin. They were like a terrified, stampeding herd of animals.

There was one little toddler, separated from his mother, sitting on the ground wailing dismally. B.-P. stopped and picked him up. A shudder of dismay ran through the crowd. But B.-P. was not going to harm him. Instead, he sat the little boy gently down on a rock, fished in his pocket and found something for him to play with. The tears stopped as the little black fist closed round the new toy. And the wailing and shuddering of the women stopped too. Here and there, a black face broke into a relieved smile. When the rest of B.-P.'s patrol caught up with him, they were amazed to find that he and his orderly were safe.

This area where Dinuzulu had taken refuge was the Ceza, a steep mountain almost on the border of the Transvaal, scarred with thickly wooded ravines and littered with boulders big enough to hide a whole patrol. The Usutus would need some winkling out of such a fortress.

B.-P. returned with as much information as he could gather about the strength of the enemy and General Smyth moved his forces into a semi-circular position round the Ceza, ready to attack. One false move and it would be all too easy for Dinuzulu to slip out of the other half of the circle and across the border into Boer territory where he would be safe from British attack. And that was exactly what happened.

Just as Smyth was ready to swoop, a message arrived from the Governor of Natal saying that no military operation could take place without his express permission. How the General fumed at the stupidity of dividing command between civil and military authorities! How frustrated B.-P. felt that his skilled work of reconnaissance was likely to be wasted! The wrangling went on for five days. When at last General Smyth was permitted to make his attack, he found there was no resistance at all. Dinuzulu and his vast army had seized their opportunity and had slipped clean away out of British territory.

B.-P. and his men combed the mountainsides. They found improvised forts and innumerable huts, all indicating that a very large force had been camping there. He found weapons in some of the forts and trinkets left behind. In the largest, he came upon a long rope of curiously carved wooden beads. Only a great chieftain would have possessed such an impressive necklace; B.-P. was convinced that it had belonged to Dinuzulu himself. He put it in his pocket as a trophy, little realising then to what use he would put the strange beads in the future.

Once again, he had seen little actual fighting but had learned much. He had had to deploy his men under genuine war conditions; he had worked with native scouts and levies. He had

had experience of guerrilla tactics in warfare and had seen the need for special skills and initiative. By September 12th, 1888 he was back at his desk in Cape Town with a gratifying promotion to the rank of Major and with his title of *Acting* Military Secretary changed to *Assistant*. Moreover, his book on pigsticking was at last published, dedicated 'by kind permission' to the Duke of Connaught. If only he could do something more interesting than his 'office job' at the Cape, life, he thought, would be very good indeed.

He had ambitious ideas of spending several months exploring the navigability of the River Zambesi and even asked his brother Warington to have a collapsible boat sent out from England for him to use where the river had stretches of rapids. However, General Smyth was not going to have his A.D.C. escaping his duties and allowed him no more than two weeks' leave so he was only able to explore for elephant. He wanted to observe them, not shoot them; all his life B.-P. felt that elephants were such magnificent and intelligent creatures that he could not bring himself to kill them.

Then it was back to the social circuit again.

Fate came to B.-P.'s rescue in the form of two months' sick leave, for he became very ill with painful carbuncles and the doctor prescribed 'patience and poultices'. During the short period in England, he came to the attention of Sir Francis de Winton who was to head a Royal Commission of Boers and British that was to sort out the confused affairs of Swaziland. As a result, Sir Francis 'borrowed' B.-P. for two months to act as his private secretary on the expedition.

Swaziland was a small upland territory adjoining Zululand and the Transvaal. White settlers had moved into the country both as farmers and prospectors. The ruling chieftain had quite happily sold the same grazing and mineral rights several times over to different settlers leading, inevitably, to disputes. The Boers were anxious to annexe the country; Britain was equally anxious to keep the peace among the native tribes in what was still a fairly sensitive area. It was decided, therefore, that a joint commission of British and Boers should work out some settlement with the Queen Regent. The unscrupulous chieftain who had caused all the trouble had conveniently died.

Sir Francis's commission went first to Pretoria to join their Boer colleagues and here B.-P. for the first time met 'Oom Paul' (as Paul Kruger was known), the suspicious and silent man who was President of the Transvaal. The party received warm hospitality from their Boer hosts which further increased the respect B.-P. already had for the Boers. It was a liking he retained even when they were fighting on opposite sides a few years later in the Boer War. He was particularly interested when he talked with the young Boers, the 'Young Afrikanders', who looked forward to a federation of all the South African states instead of endless rivalry between British and Boer. Perhaps here was sown the seed of B.-P.'s later ideal of the 'Brotherhood of Scouts' which would supersede barriers of nation and creed.

After Pretoria, there was a nine-day journey by mule-coach across the open veldt to the Swaziland capital. It was sheer delight to B.-P. Once again he donned the broad-brimmed Boer hat, the flannel-shirt and shorts he had come to find so comfortable. Each evening the Commission camped under the stars; each morning B.-P. and one or two of his companions went out shooting for the pot — snipe, partridge, duck. Except on Sundays. The Boers permitted no shooting, no travelling, no anything else on Sundays.

It took a week to settle terms with the Queen Regent and her chieftains but at the end of that time, the independence of the Swazi nation was assured. The whole expedition was to prove an educative experience for B.-P. It showed him clearly the problems that could arise from the unscrupulous exploitation of native peoples. It also showed him that patient negotiation could settle problems better than a show of arms. This was to influence his thinking in the future for, although he was a soldier by profession, he was at heart a man of peace. He has been described as 'a bad hater'. In all his writings, there are no harsh words about an enemy unless he was guilty of cruelty — but that, whether towards men or women, towards children or animals, always roused him to anger.

When the Commission arrived in Natal at the conclusion of its task, B.-P. found a letter from his uncle, General Smyth, announcing that he had been appointed Governor of Malta and inviting his nephew to join him there as Military Secretary and A.D.C. The letter, though affectionate, contained a hint that the General's patience was wearing a little thin with his enterprising and ambitious relative:

... and I have some provisos to lay down — viz. if you

come, you will have to look to my work only for your career, and to fitting yourself for that work for your employment whilst with me; and you will have to give up the expectation of leave for extraneous objects, whether political, sporting, or exploratory, unless only for a few days, or unless I be going on leave myself . . .

B.-P. wired his acceptance of the position *and* his agreement to the provisos. He must for the moment have forgotten his sense of frustration with the Staff job in Cape Town! That he remembered too late showed in a letter home. 'Did I do rightly?' he asked.

CHAPTER 5

Mediterranean Adventures

THE NEWLY KNIGHTED General Sir Henry Smyth had only been Governor of Malta for three months when his restless A.D.C. was fidgeting to be getting into action once more in yet another part of his beloved Africa. Sir Francis de Winton had asked if he could 'borrow' B.-P. again for service in Uganda. 'I cannot promise a war,' he wrote 'but we shall have to . . . replace Mwanga.' Sir Henry put his foot down. He was not prepared to lend his A.D.C. to Sir Francis de Winton or, indeed, to anyone else. He had spelled out the conditions when he offered his nephew the appointment in Malta and B.-P. had accepted them.

'You can't picture that "camp sickness" (as I should call it) that gets hold of one,' he wrote unhappily to his mother. 'A sort of hunger to be out in the wilds and away from all this easy-going mixture of office, drawing-room, clerk and butler . . .'

As senior A.D.C. he was responsible for all the Governor's and Lady Smyth's entertaining — not just of the Maltese, British and Italian communities on the island but of the senior personnel of all naval vessels, British and foreign, that paid courtesy visits. There were private visitors to entertain in the shape of wealthy yacht-owners who included a call at Malta in their Mediterranean cruises. As Military Secretary he was responsible for liaison with the five British regiments stationed on the island; with the reception and despatch of official mail; and so on and so on. There was plenty to keep him busy but was it leading anywhere?

He was beginning to realise that the two spells as A.D.C., though giving him social opportunities, were not of any assistance in advancing him in his profession. If he was ever to achieve high rank in the army, B.-P. must either spend two years at Staff College or else qualify for staff work without college by doing actual service in the field. So far, participation in any real action had eluded him; he seemed only to arrive in time for the 'mopping up' operations. (It is interesting that B.-P. and his great contemporary Winston Churchill both shared this frustration — and both subsequently achieved fame at the same time) B.-P. decided the only thing to do was to try to get into Staff College so he wrote home reluctantly for books on the hated arithmetic, algebra and geometry. He also studied Italian, the language of a large proportion of Malta's population; he could not tolerate an aimless existence.

Inevitably, there were theatricals to arrange to keep up the morale of the troops, for boredom was as much a problem in Malta as in India. There were no films or TV for the troops in the 1890s. Everything had to be devised and improvised on the spot. Out came *Cox & Box* again and all the plays he had taken out to India in 1876. Out came the scripts and music for the Gilbert & Sullivan operas. If B.-P. himself appeared frequently on the boards, it was because there was such a shortage of performers or because an artiste let him down at the last moment. One such occasion was when a dancer who had been billed to perform the Can-Can (then all the rage) failed to turn up. Always good for a lark, B.-P. himself donned the voluminous pleated skirt and 'brought the house down' with his high kicks. He used to say in later life that the nimble feet he acquired in his 'skirt dance' enabled him to escape at speed over the rocks when he was pursued in the Matoppo Hills in 1896!

As a general rule, admission to such concerts would have been free but B.-P. insisted on making a nominal charge, the proceeds of which he set aside in a special fund. After two years he had gathered together enough in entrance fees to rent a disused hospital in Valetta which he turned into a social club for non-commissioned officers and men. There was an outcry from local publicans who thereby lost the men's custom; there was an equally loud outcry from the service chaplains who protested at the club's location in the worst part of the town. 'But if you had an infected place on your body,' B.-P. asked them, 'where would you put the poultice?' And the club was nicknamed 'The Poultice' thereafter.

Sir Henry devised a method of keeping his restless A.D.C happy. It so happened that the position of Intelligence Officer for the Mediterranean (based on Malta) fell vacant. Knowing B.-P.'s talent for reconnaissance (and knowing also that he would be tempted to go off on unofficial wild adventures anyway!), Sir Henry nominated B.-P. for the appointment and it was approved. The position brought no pay — B.-P. would still have to manage on his meagre allowance of fifteen shillings (75p) per day — but it offered promise of adventure and it would also be another way of serving his country. Patriotism is considered somewhat out-dated today when the world has shrunk. Civilisation has become so sophisticated that a minor dispute in one part of the world can affect the economics and stability of all the rest. In Queen Victoria's reign, the issues seemed simpler and B.-P. was, in his respect for his Queen and his love of his country, very much a man of his times.

As Intelligence Officer, he was responsible for collecting and passing on to the War Office information regarding the ships and troops of different countries, their armament and any other information that could possibly be of military value. He used many devices to justify his presence in the neighbourhood of various military targets and manoeuvres; he did not repeat his mistakes of Krasnoe Selo. Thus, he rowed idly past the forts guarding the Dardanelles, ostensibly fishing, but in fact observing the angle and placing of the gun embrasures. He went snipe-shooting at Bizerta as a cover for watching the build-up of the big French naval base in Tunis. He visited Algeria as a tourist and observed the manoeuvres of the crack French Spahis and Chasseurs d'Afrique. A steady flow of plans, sketches and maps reached the War Office in London from his busy pen.

On one occasion, following rumours that some particularly powerful new guns had been installed by the Turks in a fort commanding the Bosphorus, B.-P. was instructed to secure details. He took an American lady friend in Constantinople into his confidence and told her how anxious he was to get inside one of the forts.

'That's easy,' said his friend. 'I know Hamid Pasha who is stationed in one of them. He told me I could go and have tea with him any time I wanted.'

Hamid Pasha proved to be a charming host. He showed the American lady and her friend all over the fort and finally indicated its guns shrouded in canvas covers. B.-P.'s excitement was intense! Evidently assuming that both his visitors were American, the Turk flung back the covers. B.-P. gasped; they were the same old guns that had been in the fort for years!

'You see,' said Hamid Pasha, 'we are trying to impress a certain power with the idea that we are re-arming our forts. If there are any spies around, they will think that we have new guns under these covers.'

These exploits may sound 'cloak and dagger' stuff compared with the sinister and sophisticated network of espionage that exists today but, even eighty-odd years ago, they required none the less courage and imagination of a high order.

One of B.-P.'s best-known and most daring exploits took place in Dalmatia, at that time part of the powerful Austro-Hungarian Empire. B.-P. wished to ascertain particulars of the fort at Cattaro. With his usual attention to detail, he acquired all the paraphernalia of a butterfly hunter — net, killing bottle and so forth. He also prepared a sketch-book with several completed drawings and paintings of butterflies and a few others in outline only. Thus equipped, he climbed the barren Krivosi heights above Cattaro and began to commit his observations of the fort to paper. Whenever he was challenged, he displayed his sketch-book and asked whether this, that or the other butterfly was to be found in that neighbourhood. As very few people know anything at all about butterflies (as, indeed, B.-P. himself did not!) his drawings passed muster. Had the challengers examined the drawings closely, they would have seen that in the later drawings, the delicate lines outlined the plan of the fort and the veins running across the wings led from the positions of the guns on the plan to notes of their calibre disguised as spots on the butterfly's wings.

On another occasion, he wanted to watch the Italian army's manoeuvres in mountainous territory. He entered the country from Switzerland and put up for the night at a mountain inn. Very early in the morning, he climbed up to what he guessed would be a vantage point to view the manoeuvres. Reaching the top of a ridge, he was startled to see how close was the Mont Blanc massif and how beautiful it looked as the sun came up: '. . . the wonderful red light on the mountain was reflected on the surface of the glaciers although they themselves were still in the greeny-blue stage.' He could see the twinkling of numerous camp-fires and realised that the Italian troops were bivouacked below him. He was at a suitable place to watch any activity, so he sat down and allowed the artist in him to enjoy capturing in water-colour the magnificent view of the mountains. He was in the midst of painting when he saw two columns of soldiers approaching. He went on with his painting, just tossing off a casual 'Good morning!' in Italian as they passed. Two officers came across to find out who he was and why he was there. B.-P. showed them his painting of 'Dawn Among the Mountains'. It was so obviously a talented piece of work that any suspicions the officers might have had about B.-P. now disappeared. They chatted for a while and he asked them casually about their own reasons for being on the mountains so early in the day.

'The less interest I showed,' he wrote later, 'the more keen they seemed to be to explain matters to me, until eventually I had the whole scheme exposed before me, illustrated by their own sketch maps of the district, which were far more detailed and complete than anything of the kind I had seen before.'

The butterfly hunter

After a while, the officers moved on, leaving B.-P. in peace to make all the observations he required.

After three years, Sir Henry's tour of duty as Governor of Malta came to an end. As the date of departure approached, B.-P. became increasingly anxious about his own future. His application for recognition without actual attendance at Staff College had been turned down for lack of an active service record. He had applied to be sent on various small campaigns in the Sudan and Mashonaland but these applications had also failed. His future in the army looked bleak. He wrote for advice to his old Colonel, Sir Baker Russell, and the reply was prompt and direct: 'Resign as Military Secretary in Malta. Rejoin your regiment and get in some regular service.'

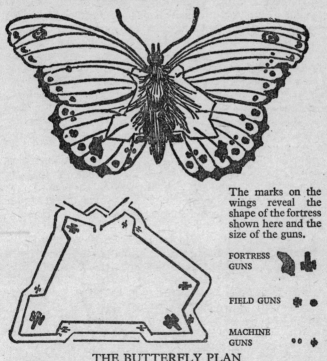

The marks on the wings reveal the shape of the fortress shown here and the size of the guns.

FORTRESS GUNS

FIELD GUNS

MACHINE GUNS

THE BUTTERFLY PLAN

Only the markings on the lines of the butterfly have any significance

He did resign and arrived back in England in May 1893 to find that his brother George, now aged forty-five, had married — the first of her sons to turn to what Mrs. Baden-Powell had dismissed as 'the selfish, ordinary life of earning and spending for himself alone'. B.-P., however, was delighted with his new sister-in-law, though he reassured his mother that he himself was 'safe' for the time being. 'I'm too young yet!' he wrote.

The 13th Hussars were stationed in Ireland and, despite his long absence, B.-P. was welcomed back warmly and resumed command of his old squadron. He worked hard at being a good regimental officer, taking his men through a musketry course and taking a veterinary course himself. The summer manoeuvres were held that year in the presence of Lord Wolseley whom B.-P. had last met in Seaforth years earlier when they tried out the 'galloping carriage' on the sand-dunes. As usual, B.-P.'s unusual methods singled him out for notice.

It was an extremely dry summer for Ireland and the roads were dusty. B.-P. had observed that the guard on the particular post he was detailed to capture always worked 'by the book' and kept watch only on the road in front of them. He detailed a sergeant and half a dozen of his troopers to cut down branches from the trees and to gallop along the road towing the branches behind them. The branches stirred up clouds of dust in the middle of which could occasionally be glimpsed a hussar uniform. The 'enemy' assumed that the whole troop was passing along the road. In the meantime, B.-P. and the rest of his detachment circled round and took the post from the rear.

Lord Wolseley was delighted. 'I like to see an officer use his wits and not always feel tied down by Drill Book regulations,' he said.

The 13th Hussars were in Ireland for two years. B.-P. resigned himself to spending the rest of his years of service with them without hope of promotion to high rank. 'I am afraid the Staff College is beyond me now,' he wrote to his brother. 'I think I am over-age and I am certain I can't afford a crammer — nor can I learn the required mathematics.'

He worked harder than ever to try to earn more money from his articles and sketches. He managed to earn £47 in one year — a considerable sum for those days. It appeared, too, that he would have an opportunity of earning even more, for the *Graphic* invited him to spend his leave as their correspondent in Turkey following on the massacres in Armenia. The pay offered seemed a princely sum: thirty shillings (£1.50) a day and all expenses paid. B.-P. wired his acceptance and began to pack.

But he did not get to Turkey on that occasion. Before he had time to complete his arrangements, Lord Wolseley sent for him. He was to go on active service to the Gold Coast. 'You will raise a native contingent,' B.-P. was told 'and command it as a scouting and pioneering force for our Ashanti expedition.' Lord Wolseley looked at the young officer and smiled. 'It's not cavalry service,' he added 'but you will have every opportunity to make full use of your wits!'

B.-P. was elated. Not only was he to go to Africa again but on *active service*. Maybe he could earn that Staff College recognition after all.

CHAPTER 6

'He-of-the-Big-Hat'

BRITAIN HAD IN all nine wars against the Ashanti during the nineteenth century. This people occupied the land beyond the Prah river which formed the northern boundary of the Gold Coast Province of equatorial Africa. They were one of the most cruel and savage of tribes; they practised human sacrifice and constantly raided neighbouring tribes to obtain victims. As the century advanced, the Ashanti grew more arrogant. On several occasions they wiped out the British forces sent against them and even when themselves defeated, they completely ignored the terms of any peace settlement.

The last expedition against them had been led by the very man who now put B.-P. in charge of native levies: the then Sir Garnet Wolseley. After his defeat of King Kofi Karikari, the Treaty of Fomena had laid down that human sacrifice must be abolished, that trade routes across Ashanti territory must be kept open and that the sum of 50,000 oz. of Ashanti gold should be paid by the King. That had been in 1873 and, needless to say, none of the terms of the treaty had been fulfilled. Now King Prempeh had succeeded 'King Coffee' on the Golden Stool of Ashanti and he was proving every bit as uncooperative as his predecessor. By 1895 the British Government had had enough; they decided that the time had come to break Prempeh completely and to endeavour to stamp out once and for all the savage practices of his people.

Lord Wolseley had selected Sir Francis Scott of the Gold Coast Constabulary as over-all leader of the expedition. B.-P. was to raise a levy of native troops to go ahead of the main force, clearing a route from Prahsu on the Gold Coast border to Prempeh's capital, Kumasi. He was also to scout for information about Prempeh and his movements. In the middle of

December 1895 B.-P. and his assistant, Capt. Graham of the 15th Lancers, landed at Cape Coast Castle on the Gold Coast and began to gather their force together.

They decided to organise their levies into companies of about 100, each with a king or chief at its head. The account books make amusing reading: '1 king @ 10s per diem', '1 chief @ 7/6d per diem', so many men '@ 9d per diem'. 'Uniform' was distributed — one red fez for each man. As the levies wore little other than a loin-cloth, a fez was all the uniform required and it seemed to give enormous pride and pleasure. B.-P. himself wore, instead of a topee, the wide-brimmed Boer hat that has come to be associated with him. It shaded his fair freckled skin and kept it from sunburn and also, to some extent, protected his face when pushing through undergrowth. The hat earned him the name among the Ashantis of 'Kantankye' which mean 'He-of-the-Big-Hat'.

As the detachment hacked its way slowly north, B.-P. had, time and again, to curb his impatience and to remember the Gold Coast proverb: 'Softly, softly, catchee monkey.' Somehow he had to *lead* this motley collection of men. He and Graham were the only two white officers for over 800 untrained, undisciplined natives. B.-P. broke down the command even further — rather after the fashion of the Patrol system he was to introduce later in Scouting — by dividing his companies into smaller groups of about twenty men, each under its own leader.

Once across the Prah and into Ashanti territory, the work became gruelling. Dense forest closed in and B.-P. had to learn new techniques as he went along. Using only machetes and axes, they had to hack a road wide enough to take the following army through fifty miles of jungle. They had to lay 'corduroy' or log roads over swamps, they had to bridge innumerable streams, clear areas for camps and build rest huts and stores for equipment — all in the humid, stifling twilight of tropical forest. There was always a very real danger of attack by the Ashanti but an even greater danger for white men from fever. Capt. Graham fell ill and had to be replaced; his substitute also succumbed, and the next, and the next. In all, B.-P. had five replacements and all went down with malaria or dysentery. He himself kept going — which he attributed to the fact that he always carried a spare shirt tied on by the sleeves. As soon as the one he was wearing became soaked with sweat, he changed it for the dry one, allowing the first shirt to dry again.

Building bridges in Ashanti

One of his substitute officers for a time was a Major Gordon of the 15th Hussars. He was working on a parallel road to B.-P.'s some three or four miles away. It happened that one of the native scouts killed a goat to supplement the service rations. Wishing to share this luxury with Gordon, B.-P. hacked off a large portion and sent it by native runner. It had a label attached on which was written 'Major Gordon' and the date on which the goat was killed, just in case its delivery was delayed. The drill was that Gordon would initial the label and return it to B.-P. to indicate the safe receipt of the meat. However, by the time the runner had returned, B.-P. and his working party had already moved on, so the runner delivered the label to one of the officers leading the van of Sir Francis Scott's army which was following close behind. Consternation! 'Major Gordon killed . . .' The message passed swiftly back down the line by field telegraph to H.Q. 'Major Gordon has been killed.' Back up the line came the questions to B.-P. 'Where had the battle taken place?' 'Why had B.-P. sent in no report?' What a misunderstanding that small label had caused!

The road pushed forward through the jungle, over the Adansi Hills and eventually, more quickly as the forest thinned, down into the open clearing where Kumasi lay — hardly a 'city' in the European sense but rather a collection of wattle and daub huts with the 'Palace' at the rear. This was a collection of much larger and more imposing huts, connected by a series of courts.

There was no resistance — only the throbbing and booming of 'drum talk' as B.-P. and his levies moved cautiously into a large open space, rather like a vast parade-ground, in front of the palace. Could it be that King Prempeh realised that he was outnumbered? The square began to fill. Men, women and children came out of the huts. A band approached, beating drums and playing on horns made out of elephant tusks. A procession of chiefs followed, colourful with their bobbing state umbrellas. Finally King Prempeh was carried in and lowered on his throne to the ground. He wore a black and gold tiara on his head and a necklace and bracelets of pure gold round his throat and arms. Not a word was uttered. He sat there, silent and inscrutable, waiting for Sir Francis Scott and his forces. He sat there, still inscrutable, as those forces marched into the square — two thousand British troops, twelve thousand native carriers, column after column after column.

Sir Francis and his officers seated themselves in a semi-circle before Prempeh and commanded him to approach and hear what message they brought from the British Government. The atmosphere was tense. Would this be the signal for an Ashanti attack?

Still without a word, Prempeh rose and approached the British leader. He listened in silence as Sir Francis told him that the Governor would be arriving in a few days' time and that the King would have to make submission to him. He listened in silence as he was told that he must produce the 50,000 oz. of Ashanti gold still unpaid from the Treaty of Fomena. Still without a word or a flicker of expression, Prempeh turned when Sir Francis had finished and stalked back to his throne. The bearers lifted it shoulder high and carried him away in the same manner as he had come.

It was all too easy. What was Prempeh plotting? B.-P. and his scouts decided to do a little investigation for themselves. Exploration showed that there was one point behind the palace enclosure where the bush had not been cleared. There was a hardly noticeable door in the palace stockade through which anyone inside could escape unseen into the cover of the bush and so away from the city to the security of the forest beyond.

B.-P.'s first precaution was to clear the bush so that there was an open path all round the palace enclosure which no-one could cross unobserved. Then he concealed sentries round the whole area and maintained a twenty-four-hour watch.

For two days and nights nothing happened. Arrangements went ahead for the ceremony of Prempeh's submission to the Governor. B.-P. guessed that if anything was going to happen, it would be the night before the ceremony. He made his plans accordingly.

As dusk fell, Prempeh's chiefs and counsellors, one by one, approached and entered the royal palace. Hours passed; it seemed to be a long palaver. A steamy mist added to the sinister atmosphere. From where he lay hidden, B.-P. could scarcely even see the secret door in the palace stockade.

In the early hours, he was alerted by a figure emerging stealthily through the mist from the direction of the door. He let the figure pass then gave a low whistle, the signal arranged with his men behind him. Sounds of sudden movement. A gasp. A grunt. Silence. Another figure slipped out of the palace and again the procedure was repeated. Prempeh's chieftains, far from escaping to bring up their troops to surprise the British, were themselves being ambushed and gagged and bound.

One of the last of the Ashanti to leave the palace stopped just by B.-P. Something had alerted him to danger. He stood perfectly still, suspicious, like a stag scenting his hunters. He turned, as if to run back to the palace to give warning. B.-P. rose from his hiding-place, grabbed the Ashanti round the neck from behind and tumbled him to the ground. They wrestled furiously, B.-P. struggling to get a grip on the smoothly oiled body of his opponent. The native broke loose and grabbed his gun, swinging it like a club, but at that moment help arrived and that Ashanti also was overpowered and put with the other prisoners.

The following morning, his plan of escape foiled, King Prempeh had to make his submission to Governor Maxwell. There was no intention to depose him, the Governor assured him. The British army had come merely to ensure that the terms of the Treaty were observed. If King Prempeh would cease troubling the neighbouring tribes, if he would stop human sacrifices, if he would keep open the new road that B.-P. had cleared through the forest, he could rule in peace. *And* there was the question of the 50,000 oz. of gold; it must be paid at once. Impossible, declared the King, speaking for the first time. 680 oz. was the most he could produce! The Governor was convinced he was lying and B.-P. was detailed to organise a search for the gold.

He and his men turned Kumasi upside down but they never did find the Ashanti gold — it was too well hidden. Nor did they find Prempeh's 'golden stool' or his golden chair of state. What they did find was Prempeh's fetish grove. The ground under the owa-owa trees was heaped with skeletons of decapitated bodies — sure confirmation that human sacrifice was still practised by the Ashantis.

B.-P. also found a vast bowl of beaten brass, about eighteen inches deep. He decided it would make an excellent camp bath and ordered it to be put with his kit. He changed his mind about bathing in it, however, when he learned it was the 'fetish bowl' in which the Ashanti used to collect the blood of their victims!

Once again, mercifully, it had turned out to be a bloodless war; and it had reinforced many theories that B.-P. was later to develop and use with great effect: the need for practical skills and a sensible care of the health, the importance of leadership, the value of delegated responsibility — even the value of a six-foot surveying pole which, Capt. Graham had demonstrated, could be used for pole-jumping streams and probing the depth of swamp as well as for simple measuring.

He was scarcely back in Ireland with the regiment and with now the Brevet rank of Lieutenant-Colonel than he was posted back to Africa, this time to deal with a rising of the Matabele tribe.

CHAPTER 7

'The-Wolf-That-Never-Sleeps'

THE MATABELE WERE really Zulus who had been cut off from their original territory when the Boers made their Great Trek into the Transvaal in 1836. Much of the story of the southern half of the African continent recalls the Border feuds of the fourteenth and fifteenth centuries between the Welsh and the English. The problems of South Africa were not really political but economic. Where prosperity depended on cattle, each tribe needed land to graze its beasts. The inter-tribal wars and uprisings that took place throughout the nineteenth century were very much like the cattle-raiding expeditions and reprisals along the Welsh border that gave rise to the nursery rhyme:

> Taffy was a Welshman, Taffy was a thief;
> Taffy came to my house and stole a piece of beef . . .
> I went to Taffy's house, Taffy was in bed.
> I took up a poker and flung it at his head.

In this instance, the Matabele, driven from their own lands by the Boers, had gone to the Shona's 'house' and had appropriated the territory of this peaceable tribe in the south of what is now Rhodesia.

In that name, 'Rhodesia', lay the seeds of this present uprising.

Cecil Rhodes, a brilliant, wealthy man, had become Prime Minister of Cape Colony in 1890. It was his ambition to extend British influence over the whole of Africa and, in particular, to join the Cape to Cairo by railway. In the scramble for central Africa, he was anxious to secure the territory of the Matabele and the Mashonas before either Germany or Portugal could do so for thereby either of those countries would have a strip of possessions right across the continent, effectively cutting off South Africa from the north.

Rhodes made a decidedly sharp agreement with the Matabele king which gave Rhodes's mining company control over the mineral rights of 75,000 square miles of Matabele territory in exchange for £100 cash, 1,000 rifles, 100,000 cartridges and a steamboat on the Zambesi! It was not until miners poured into the country by the thousand, taking over good cattle grazing land for their camps and mines, that the Matabele king realised he had been duped.

But, as so often happens when men achieve great power, Rhodes over-reached himself. His agent in the northern part of the new 'Rhodesia' quite unlawfully led a raid into the Transvaal with the idea of helping non-Boer settlers to demand their rights. This was the ill-fated 'Jameson Raid' which implicated Rhodes and toppled him from power. This was the cue the Matabele needed. They were already in desperate straits as there had been a disastrous drought which, along with a disease called 'rinderpest', was killing off all their cattle. If the white men, Rhodes and Jameson, were not after all as powerful as they had seemed, perhaps the Matabele could drive out *all* the white settlers and take back their land for grazing again.

They consulted their god, the M'limo, who told them to massacre all the white people in Bulawayo and afterwards to slaughter all those in the outlying farms. In their enthusiasm, the Matabele carried out the oracle's instructions in the wrong order: they attacked the farms first. Consequently, the citizens of Bulawayo had time to prepare their defences. This was the situation in the late spring of 1896 which brought Colonel Plumer hurrying from the Cape at the head of 800 British troops and General Sir Frederick Carrington and his force from England, with Lieut.-Col. Robert S. S. Baden-Powell as his Chief-of-Staff.

They had a formidable task ahead of them. The area covered by the uprising was as big as France, Spain and Italy together. There were no railways and no proper roads and it was estimated that there were 12,000 Matabele against 2,000 British. The use of disciplined troops, however, inflicted quick defeats on the Matabele who, feeling that the M'limo's magic did not work against foreign soldiers, began to lose heart. It soon became apparent that their *impis* were withdrawing to the Matoppo Hills and that, if they were to be driven from this tangle of rock and ravine, detailed information, guides and maps would be needed. Inevitably the task was entrusted to B.-P.

He teamed up with an American scout, Major Fred Burnham who had lived for many years in the area. Together they reconnoitred the enemy positions. The Englishman learned a lot from the American about 'reading signs' — tricks that Burnham had learned from the Red Indians. B.-P. would also prowl alone at night, locating the enemy camping grounds and estimating their strength by the number of their camp-fires — a habit which earned him the name among the Matabele of 'Impeesa' — 'The-Wolf-That-Never-Sleeps'. He would creep among the rocks, lying low, pausing, inching forward again with infinite patience, knowing it was a deadly game of hide-and-seek he was playing; knowing also that his own safety and that of the army back in camp depended on his skill in reconnaissance. Once he was spotted by a Matabele sentry and it was a case of who could run faster over the rough boulders and slipping stones. B.-P. wore rubber-soled shoes for these expeditions, both for quietness and for speed, and he swore his skill at 'skirt-dancing' in the regimental concert in Malta enabled him to be more nimble than the enemy!

On four occasions he led Col. Plumer's troops to attack rebel strongholds and on each occasion brought them right out on top of the enemy — but they were no nearer quelling the rebellion. By the middle of June, the Mashonas had joined in. More troops were sent from the Cape. B.-P. was transferred completely on to the work of reconnaissance and took as his companion a young Zulu named Jan Grootboom who had a high reputation for his skill as a scout. He spoke good English and usually wore European clothes. They would ride by night into enemy territory, have a brief sleep, then lie up during the day studying the enemy positions, his supplies, the whereabouts of his cattle and any other information of use. As night approached, they would return again to base — always by a different route — to make their report.

One early morning, they were close to an enemy camp waiting for the morning cooking fires to give away the size and extent of the force before them. At dawn, first one fire was lit, then another, and another.

'The swine,' muttered Grootboom. 'They know we are here and are laying a trap for us.'

He whispered to B.-P. that he would go and investigate and, stripping off his European clothes, crept off, every inch a naked savage. B.-P. waited and waited for him to return. Had he turned traitor? It was one of the penalties of the job, B.-P. would admit, that spying made one suspicious even of one's friends. He moved his position to a more secure hiding place and waited. After an hour, he saw Grootboom returning and felt bitterly ashamed of his doubts. The Zulu had been correct in his suspicions. He had found a large party of Matabele waiting to ambush them as they returned. What had alerted Grootboom's suspicions was the fact that the fires had been lit one after another in regular sequence, as if a single man was running from one to another. If they had been genuine cooking fires, they would have sprung up irregularly — a lesson for B.-P. in observation and deduction.

The campaign proceeded with infuriating slowness. The best successes were when the enemy could be lured or driven out of his established village which was then destroyed. The British forces were divided into a number of small flying columns which could move at speed and between them cover large areas of territory. Gradually, the Matabele were driven deeper into the mountains, leaving behind their herds and their women and children. But the Matoppos was an impossible area for military operations. When an *impi* was driven from one place, it simply moved further into the mountains. However, questioning of prisoners indicated that even the Matabele leaders themselves were growing weary of the campaign. B.-P. asked permission to try out a 'dodge', as he called it.

At the beginning of August, he and Grootboom had taken prisoner two women, one of whom, a very aged crone, turned out to be a close relative of the Matabele chief. On August 11th, the old lady was taken to the mountains and set down more or less where the Chief's kraal had stood. A hut was built for her and she was provided with food and a woman attendant. A big white flag was erected above the hut. Before they withdrew, the two native troops who had undertaken this part of the 'dodge' shouted to the rebels (who they knew were watching them from the rocks) that if they wanted peace, they should come down and talk to the old lady; she would have all the information. They had four days in which to make up their minds. In the meantime, the British would make no attack.

During the night, the two women and the flag disappeared. Nothing happened for one day, two days, three. On the morning of the fourth day, the flag had reappeared and with it a message that the chieftains would like to talk over the terms of surrender with 'the white chief'. But which white chief? General Carrington? The High Commissioner? In the end, Cecil Rhodes, with great personal courage, offered to go unarmed into the Matoppos for an *indaba* or conference with the chieftains. Thus the first steps were taken towards what became known as 'Rhodes's Peace'.

B.-P. meantime was sent on 'mopping up' operations against natives who were still fighting in the north. Usually he found that the enemy had already fled at their approach and he would find abandoned camps with clothing, tools and tinned provisions obviously looted from murdered whites. Once he found a sort of trumpet made from the twisted horn of a koodoo, a species of antelope, which he decided to keep as a souvenir. For the most, however, it was a tedious and arduous task, involving long treks over the plateau in hardship, discomfort and scorching heat, with veldt sores and fatigue, with dreadful thirst when streams and waterholes were found to be dried up, with scanty and unpalatable food such as boiled horse because the game they expected to supply them was infected with rinderpest.

At last there remained only one *impi* to be subjugated: that of the chief Wedza. It took a long, weary trek of over 120 miles of veldt before they reached his mountain stronghold and it was the pattern of the Matoppos all over again — how to winkle out the chieftain and his *impi* from a secure position — particularly when B.-P. had no more than 115 men?

He remembered Jan Grootboom and the Matabele cooking fires and decided to improve on that ruse. He must turn his 115 men into a much larger force. Throughout the day, his handful of men played a game of deception. Intermittent bursts of gunfire came from one side and then from another. A group of twenty-five men were despatched to the far side of the stronghold with instructions to act as if they were 250! When night fell, the Matabele looked down on hundreds of British camp-fires not lit one after another, but appearing at random as half-a-dozen men moved around lighting them. In the face of such a vast British force, how could Wedza make a stand? Dawn saw an empty stronghold. Wedza and his men had disappeared into the hills and gave no more opposition. The Matabele campaign was over.

CHAPTER 8

Genesis of an Idea

THE ARMY HAS some odd customs. An officer may hold two ranks at once. One is his 'substantive' rank on which his pay is based; the other rank is higher but temporary and is called his 'brevet' rank which gives him seniority of authority but no extra pay.

B.-P. had been awarded the brevet of full colonel for his part in the Matabele campaign, although his substantive rank was still only that of major. Thus the invidious position arose when he returned to the 13th Hussars in Ireland that although he was substantively only the third most senior officer in the regiment, his *brevet* colonelcy put him above the Regiment's *substantive* lieutenant-colonel who, until B.-P.'s return had been in command of the regiment! The War Office solved this peculiar situation by offering B.-P. command of the 5th Dragoon Guards in India.

The 5th Dragoon Guards were a mixed lot of men. They needed pulling into shape before they became a 'regiment'. Coming to the command from the outside instead of progressing through the regiment to reach command made B.-P.'s task particularly delicate. 'New brooms' are not always welcome. But he had learned a great deal in the years he had spent in Africa and Malta. He had learned how to lead men and he had learned also that the best way of getting people to do things is to make them *want* to do those things.

India had not changed. There was still the same danger of disease as there had been in the Seventies when he had been a raw sub-lieutenant. Now, in 1897, he arrived in Meerut to find enteric fever rampant among the men, with serious loss of life. It did not take him long to guess that the infection was picked up from the food and drink the men purchased in the bazaars.

He did not, however, want to issue a General Order forbidding anyone to go into the bazaar; that would have antagonised the men and even encouraged some of them to defy the order. Instead, he paraded the whole regiment, explained his theory as to the source of the infection and asked their co-operation to prove or disprove his theory by staying away from the bazaars for two weeks. With such an approach, the men co-operated willingly and there was soon a dramatic fall in the number of fever cases in the 5th.

Now the question was how to *keep* the men out of the bazaars. B.-P. opened a social club with facilities for drinks and meals and games. He found one soldier who had been a pastry-cook in England and set him to making cakes and baking bread. He set up a soft-drinks factory. He started a regimental dairy which produced its own sterilised milk and cream and butter. In addition, he was determined to turn his Dragoons into first-class soldiers. So few of them seemed to have any initiative or what he called 'guts for adventure'. He decided to put into effect the ideas he had formed on the training of men. First of all, the training should be enjoyable. Secondly, remembering his experience in the Ashanti campaign, it should be carried out in small groups, preferably in competition with one another. Last of all, it should encourage self-discipline and self-reliance.

He knew from experience that reconnaissance and scouting embraced all these ideas. Even though his service in the Matabele campaign had been arduous and dangerous, he still considered it as 'the best time of my life'. He had enjoyed the excitement and the challenge. So he started to give lectures on reconnaissance to small groups of volunteers, which soon developed into large groups. He spiced his lectures with anecdotes and illustrations from his own experience and it is easy to imagine how an actor of his ability would be able to dramatise his adventures as a spy in the Mediterranean area or would be able to impersonate the various characters he had encountered in Africa.

After the lectures, the men were given practical instruction in scouting skills over varied country and those that qualified were given the title of 'scout' and were proud to wear on the sleeve of their uniform a distinguishing badge in the shape of a fleur-de-lys, based on the design used to indicate north on a map or compass.

*Scouts of the 5th Dragoon Guards on manoeuvre. Notice First
Class badge on the right sleeve of the top-most figure.*

'Our colonel doesn't half work us hard,' one of the 5th was
heard to remark, 'but the worst of it is, we don't crack up with
hard work. We seem to be better for it!'

Everyone always spoke with affection and respect of B.-P. as
an officer. It was surely because he brought the personal touch
to his relationships. He knew every man and every officer per-
sonally, knew his family background, why he had joined the
Army and so on.

It was this relationship that brought about such excellent
discipline, because each man desired to please. This was a far
better method than discipline imposed by means of regulations
and punishments.

Of course, India meant polo again. As a full colonel, B.-P.
was now able to afford two beautiful Arab ponies and on these
he played better than ever.

Polo, like his experiences in action in Africa, was beginning to reinforce Dr. Haig Brown's first lesson in tactics:

I have often urged my young friends, when faced with an adversary, to 'play polo' with him [B.-P. was to write many years later] i.e., not to go at him bald-headed but to ride side by side with him and gradually edge him off your track. Never lose your temper with him. If you are in the right, there is no need to; if you are in the wrong you can't afford to.

In the Inter-Regimental Polo Tournament his team lost only to the 4th Hussars. There was a dinner in the evening at which everyone toasted everyone else and the guests became extremely mellow. There were many speeches — all on the subject of polo — and very late in the evening, a young member of the 4th Hussars' team rose to his feet and declared that he, too, was going to address the company on the subject.

'Sit down!' everybody shouted, but the young Hussar took no notice and proceeded to speak at length and with such eloquence that soon the noisy table fell silent and everyone listened with attention. The speech ended to loud applause — and then the orator was firmly seized by his brother officers and sat upon!

'You won't keep me down,' defied the officer. 'I'm india-rubber. I bounce!'

As indeed he continued to do for the rest of his life, for the young polo-playing Hussar was the twenty-three-year-old Winston Spencer Churchill, later to become Prime Minister of England in the darkest hours of World War II.

B.-P. spent two years in India on this tour. They were interesting years, filled with all the various activities and skills he had mastered over his forty-two years: training his men, riding, painting, writing, acting. He has been criticised for 'losing his dignity' in taking part in theatricals, particularly when a full colonel, but this criticism shows lack of understanding. He could show dignity whenever it was required and never lacked authority over his men. They *respected* his authority but they *loved* him because he was prepared occasionally to play the fool, to show a lively sense of humour and an understanding of *their* point of view.

An example of this took place in a regimental concert in

Meerut. One Private Brown took the stage to sing a solo. He was a miserable-looking specimen of a trooper; his voice was flat, he forgot his words and altogether his turn was a disaster. The audience of troops grew restless. 'Take him off!' they shouted. At this Private Brown stopped singing. He came down to the footlights looking hurt and addressed his audience above the catcalls. He was only trying to do his best, he complained. It wasn't fair. He moaned on with a string of complaints about India, the army, the regiment. And if they had a colonel like his ... Suddenly one of the young officers jumped up.

'By Jove! It's the C.O.!' he shouted. And, of course, he was right. The whining private on the stage was indeed the regiment's commanding officer. How the troops cheered him!

B.-P. had an almost obsessive compulsion for work. His early training, the friendly but fierce competition between the Baden-Powell brothers, the constant financial pressures made him use every available minute. While in India he began to jot down some of the ideas he had gathered together on the subject of reconnaissance. He gave the projected book the title *Aids to Scouting*. However, he had to set it aside for a while as his regiment was due on manoeuvres and after that were to move to a new station in the Punjab. B.-P. settled them into their fresh quarters and set off for England to take some much overdue leave. He expected to be back in India before the end of the year — but it was to be many, many years before he saw that country again, and then no longer as a soldier.

CHAPTER 9

Hero of Mafeking

B.-P. ARRIVED HOME in the middle of June 1899, but London was different on this leave. For one thing, there was a gap in the close-knit family. George, the brother with whom B.-P. had always been closest and to whom he had always turned for advice, had died but a few months before at the early age of fifty-one. It was different, too, in that there was war in the air.

Ever since gold had been discovered on the Rand, there had been unrest in the Transvaal. Non-Boer labour had flooded into the country to work the mines. This labour produced five-sixths of the revenue of the Transvaal and outnumbered the Boers by two to one, yet they had no rights. President Kruger's government steadfastly refused them the vote. It was in support of the cause of these 'Uitlanders' or foreigners that Jameson had made his ill-advised 'Raid' in 1896. Moreover, conditions in the Transvaal were becoming more and more repressive. There was no free press, judges were peremptorily dismissed and the police were given excessive powers. There were all the signs that the Transvaal was no longer a free and democratic state. Moreover, President Kruger was arming heavily and had entered into an alliance with the Orange Free State.

The British High Commissioner, Sir Alfred Milner, warned the government in London that war was inevitable. He asked that more troops and armaments be sent out from England to Cape Colony in readiness for war or maybe to prevent any actual hostilities by a show of strength. This request was rejected. The ambition was still to achieve a union of the states in South Africa; a show of strength by Britain might put back 'union' for a generation. More important, the parliament of Cape Colony had a Dutch majority.

In March 1899, twenty thousand British 'Uitlanders' in the Transvaal petitioned Queen Victoria to intervene on their behalf and a conference was called in June between President Kruger and the British High Commissioner to discuss the problem. There were only slender chances of success and the British High Command began to realise that if war did come, they were totally unprepared.

Two weeks after his return from India, B.-P. was lunching at the Naval and Military Club in London when Lord Wolseley's A.D.C. came over to him.

'Hullo,' he said. 'I thought you were in India. I've just cabled you to come home. The C.-in-C. wants to see you.'

B.-P. hurried through his lunch and reported to the War Office. Lord Wolseley came straight to the point.

'I want you to go to South Africa,' he said.

'Very good, sir,' replied B.-P.

'Can you leave next Saturday?'

'No, sir.'

The C.-in-C. looked dangerous. 'Why not?' he demanded.

'Because there's not a boat on Saturday, sir,' replied B.-P., 'but I could go on Friday.'

The C.-in-C. burst out laughing. The reply was so typical of B.-P. — always one step ahead in information. He had guessed he might be required in South Africa and had quickly looked up the sailings for the Cape.

Wolseley gave him his instructions. He was:

(1) to raise two regiments of mounted infantry,
(2) in the event of war, to organise the defence of the Rhodesian and Bechuanaland frontiers and
(3) as far as possible, to keep the forces of the enemy occupied in this direction away from their own main forces.

He was to have the high-sounding title of 'Commander-in-Chief, North-West Frontier Force' and as his Chief-of-Staff he was given the Prime Minister's son, Major Lord Edward Cecil.

When he arrived at Cape Town, B.-P. found himself completely frustrated. He was refused permission by the Cape Government to recruit any troops in the Colony; he was refused permission by the G.O.C. to call on him for stores and supplies! He set off for Bulawayo to join up with the remainder

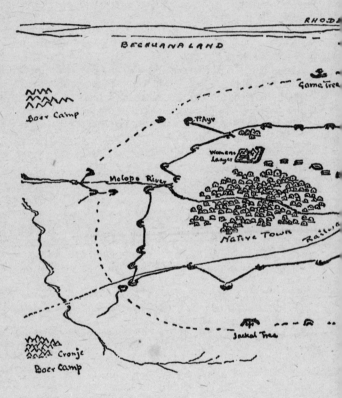

RHODE

BECHUANALAND

Game Tree

Boer Camp

ffAye

Womens
Laager

Molopo River

Native Town

Railwa

Jackal Tree

Cronje
Boer Camp

B.-P.'s own ma

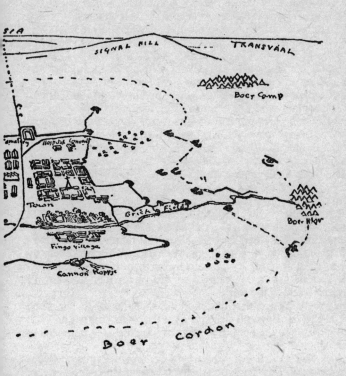

South

of Mafeking

of his staff: Col. Plumer with whom he had worked in the
Matabele campaign; Capt. McLaren who had shared his
bungalow in India way back in 1881 and Col. Hore who had
recently seen service in Egypt.

The plan they devised was a simple one. There were 500
miles of Transvaal border to keep under surveillance. Plumer,
assisted by McLaren, would raise one of the required regiments
in Rhodesia to control the northern sector; Hore would be in
charge of the second regiment, raised in Bechuanaland to the
west of the Transvaal. The only suitable base for supplies was
Mafeking on the Cape to Bulawayo railway. This town was just
inside Cape Colony at a point where that province abutted both
Bechuanaland and the Transvaal. Unfortunately, in order not
to offend the Government of Cape Colony, B.-P. could make
no overt movements towards preparing the defence of the town
and building up supplies there. Thus preparations (particularly
in building up a stock of armaments) were nowhere near complete when on October 11th the Boers declared war. B.-P. had
felt concerned that so much time had had to be spent over his
work in Mafeking instead of being able to carry out part two of
his instructions; 'to organise defence of the frontier'. He had
asked for extra troops to garrison the town but was told there
were none so he had had to call in Col. Hore and his Bechuanaland regiment. The Boers invaded the British territory on
three sides at once, laying siege to Ladysmith and Kimberley.
By October 13th, Mafeking also was surrounded and cut off
from the rest of the world.

It so happened that one of the last things B.-P. had done
before he left England was to deliver the manuscript of his *Aids
to Scouting* to the publishers. By the time the book appeared in
the shops in November 1899, the siege of Mafeking was well
under way and B.-P.'s name was well-known, so his book was
widely read. In it he had emphasised the qualities of character
necessary for a good scout: pluck, discretion, confidence and
self-reliance. That he himself and the people of Mafeking were
demonstrating these very qualities became apparent to all as
news filtered through to England of their gallant defence of the
town.

B.-P. described the siege as 'a game of bluff from start to
finish'. A modern historian has described how the little town
'sustained a gallant siege upon a heartening diet of gaiety and
wild improvisation'.

Pluck was certainly needed. The town straddled the Molopo river and covered an area of some 1,000 yards square in the middle of open veldt. There were absolutely no natural defences except one small kopje, 200 feet high, on the southern edge of the town. The railway bisected the town at right angles to the river, separating the native quarter from the rest. Inside Mafeking there were 1,500 white and 8,000 native civilians and a garrison totalling 1,251 made up of troops, police, railway officials and the Town Guard. The sole armaments consisted of 576 magazine rifles, slightly more Martin-Henry single-loaders, four seven-pounder guns, one one-pounder gun, one Nordenfelt machine-gun and eleven Maxims. B.-P. had managed to create a six-mile perimeter of 'forts' around the town but these were only made of sandbags. However, at least they would keep the Boer artillery at a distance — which would certainly be needed, for against this pitiful defence were ranged 9,000 Boers, all magnificent marksmen, all equipped with good rifles and, in the way of artillery, the latest weapons from the Krupp and Creusot works.

Discretion was also needed. B.-P. had to handle the civilian population tactfully and enlist their support, particularly as the siege dragged on and food became scarce.

Confidence was needed, not only in the face of such overwhelming odds but also the gay confidence that would keep up the spirits of the defenders. Hence B.-P.'s note of October 16th. On that date the first Boer shells fell in the town and at 2.15 p.m. the Boer Commander, General Cronje, sent a messenger with a flag of truce demanding the surrender of the town 'to prevent further bloodshed'. B.-P. replied that, so far, the only bloodshed was that of a chicken. He gave the messenger a glass of beer and sent him back with the answer 'no surrender'.

Similarly, after a long period of shelling, B.-P. smuggled a note through the Boer lines to Col. Plumer who was with his Rhodesia Regiment. B.-P. added a postscript: 'All well. Four hours' bombardment. One dog killed.' He little realised that Plumer would telegraph this message to England where its gay courage put heart into a country rapidly becoming dismayed as defeat followed defeat at the hands of the Boers.

It was not too difficult to get messages *out* of Mafeking. The town had indeed many Boer spies who could easily slip into the Boer lines at night. B.-P. took advantage of this fact to pass on misleading information to the enemy.

Self-Reliance. That quality was needed above all. Everything had to be improvised. For example, mine-fields were needed to protect the area surrounding the town. But there were no mines. Unabashed by such a trifle, B.-P. had notices distributed throughout the town in Dutch and English warning of mine-fields and the dangers of straying on to open land. He had his men carefully and ostentatiously carry into the 'mine-fields' flat boxes which they proceeded to bury with the utmost caution. After this elaborate charade, everyone was ordered to withdraw while B.-P. carried out 'tests'. He thrust a stick of dynamite down an ant-hole, lit the fuse and ran for cover. There was a convincing explosion and, as the dust settled, a figure on a bicycle could be seen pedalling like mad for the Boer lines — no doubt a spy reporting the laying of the mine-field and quite unaware that the 'mines' were no more than boxes of sand.

A searchlight was improvised from a biscuit tin and a lamp with an acetylene burner. The whole contraption was fixed on the top of a pole so that, after shining its beam over one part of the open ground between the lines, it could be rushed backwards and forwards to other positions to give the impression of a battery of searchlights. Here was the Matabele trick over again.

Hand grenades were devised from potted meat tins filled with dynamite and one enthusiastic fisherman found he could cast his further than anyone else by using a rod and line! The railway workshops constructed Mafeking's only big gun, 'The Wolf', using the steam-pipe of a railway engine reinforced with melted-down iron railings. An old eighteenth-century cannon was found in somebody's garden so this also was cleaned up, mounted on a wooden carriage and run out to various points around the perimeter. Once again, the ingenious railway workshops managed to improvise some cannon balls and the defenders of Mafeking were able to watch through their glasses with great amusement as they saw their first projectile roll like a cricket-ball into a Boer laager. There were no barbed-wire fences round the town but again, as a bluff, B.-P. had stakes driven into the ground at regular intervals and the troops were ordered, when crossing the ground between the stakes, to climb stiffly over purely imaginary barbed-wire. From the Boer lines, it would be impossible to see whether or not there actually was any wire. A competition was held among the civilian popu-

lation for the 'best dummy soldier'. The most realistic were
propped up in prominent positions to draw sniper fire so that
the marksmen among the defenders could spot where the fire
came from.

> Bluff the enemy with show of force as much as you like,
> [B.-P. wrote in Standing Orders to his men] but don't let
> yourself get too far out of touch with your own side without
> orders ... Do not always wait for an order, if you see the
> situation demands action. Don't be afraid to act for fear of
> making a mistake ... If you find you have made a mistake,
> carry it through nevertheless with energy. Pluck and dash
> have often changed a mistake into a success.

This may all sound like a splendid game but the realities of
the siege, despite the brave improvisations, became grim as
more houses were damaged, as the food supplies began to
dwindle. Though messages could be sneaked *out* of the town,
no relief supplies could get *in*. The railway was cut on both
sides of the town and the Boers were camped all around. Everybody was strictly rationed but, even so, all manner of ingenuity
had to be used to make the food last out. The wounded in hospital were treated to a special delicacy of 'blanc mange' made
from rice face-powder commandeered from the chemists. Any
horses that could be spared were shot for food and even the
skin, when the hair was removed, was boiled down with the
head and hooves and chopped up into a kind of brawn. The
mane and tail, incidentally, went to the hospital for stuffing
mattresses and pillows. With the horses shot, no fodder was
needed so their oats could be ground into rough flour and the
husks mixed with water to make a sort of porridge.

The boys of Mafeking from nine years up were organised by
Lord Edward Cecil into the Mafeking Cadet Corps and took
over all manner of duties such as message-carrying, orderly
work in the field kitchens, anything that could free a trained
man for combat duties. A picture of a cadet in uniform, with his
bicycle, appears on one of the special Mafeking postage stamps
printed during the siege. The other design carries B.-P.'s
head — an enthusiastic tribute to his leadership devised by his
officers and the postmaster. The town ran its own newspaper
('issued daily, shells permitting') and even printed its own
bank-notes.

The only break from unremitting watchfulness came on a Sunday which the God-fearing Boers set aside for worship. In Mafeking, Sunday was used for building up morale. General Orders stated that 'Sunday would be observed up till twelve o'clock, and after that hour as Saturday'. So, after Sunday morning church, the citizens and soldiers alike of the besieged town enjoyed sports, baby shows and theatricals into which the highly-respected Commander of the garrison entered with all his usual enthusiasm.

Christmas came. Rationing was suspended for the day and a 'sabbath day' truce with the Boers enabled everyone to relax. December 31st came and the beginning of a new century but as yet, no sign of any relief for Mafeking. Indeed, December had been the blackest month of the year for the British forces elsewhere in South Africa, with crushing defeats inflicted on the columns seeking to relieve Kimberley and Ladysmith. The worst disaster was the defeat of Sir Redvers Buller at Colenso. If only he had had the up-to-date maps of the River Tugela B.-P. had prepared in 1885 ... But those were filed away somewhere and forgotten.

In January 1900, Field-Marshal Lord Roberts, with Major-General Lord Kitchener as his Chief-of-Staff, arrived in Africa to take over direction of what now looked as if it was going to be a long war — but Mafeking was not an important place strategically; there were other more pressing matters to deal with first.

General Cronje had moved south from Mafeking with part of the besieging Boer force, leaving Generals Snijman and Botha in charge — but there were still 3,000 Boers encamped around Mafeking and stocks within the town were dwindling. The Boers also could afford to lose far more men than the small garrison in the town. Casualties inside Mafeking had been incredibly light but every trained man was precious and irreplaceable. An attempt the garrison had made to take Game Tree Fort to the north of the town had ended in disaster. It had been a brave effort to relieve the pressure on the town and at the same time to secure a little extra grazing for the natives' cattle. But the plan was leaked to the Boers and they were waiting in ambush for the attacking party. Twenty-four of B.-P.'s men were killed (including one officer), three were missing and twenty-three wounded. It was a shattering blow, particularly to morale.

In February, nearly five months after the siege had begun, a message from Lord Roberts written some weeks before was smuggled into the town. Could Mafeking hold out till the middle of May? B.-P. checked the rapidly dwindling stores and laid down even more stringent regulations about rationing. A bonus came their way in the form of a cloud of locusts. By themselves they 'had all the aroma and subtlety of chewed string' but fortunately the grocer's store in Mafeking still had a little curry powder which rendered them more appetising.

By March the siege had become something of a stalemate. The Boers continued with a daily bombardment; the British replied only at such intervals as would show they still *had* ammunition — supplies were running perilously low. News filtered through that the tide of war was turning in Britain's favour. Kimberley and Ladysmith had been relieved and General Cronje had been defeated, all towards the end of February. A relief force from the south was attempting to reach Mafeking; Plumer was pushing down towards them from the north. If they could only hold out!

On April 11th the Boers bombarded Mafeking for four hours with their big 94-pounder siege gun and attempted to rush the town. The defenders held their fire till the attack was almost upon them, then burst into a withering volley. The Boers withdrew.

Heavy rain brought an increase in sickness in the town. There were many cases of malaria. Rations sank to mere subsistence level. Once again the supplies were checked, every surviving animal assessed as to its food potential. A new ration scheme was worked out. Mafeking could last a few weeks longer.

Despite the shelling and the bitter realities of the siege, it was still a gentlemanly war. On the last day of April, B.-P. received a note from Sarel Eloff, one of President Kruger's thirty-five grandsons, who was in charge of a Boer Commando newly arrived to support the besieging force. The letter invited B.-P. to field a cricket team from Mafeking to play a Boer team on the following Sunday — a breach of Sunday observance as remarkable as the letter! B.-P. sent over his reply under flag of truce:

Sir, I beg to thank you for your letter of yesterday, in

which you propose that your men come and play cricket with us.

I should like nothing better — after the match in which we are at present engaged is over. But just now we are having our innings and have so far scored 200 days, not out, against the bowling of Cronje, Snijman, Botha and Eloff: and we are having a very enjoyable game.

I remain, yours truly,
R. S. S. Baden-Powell

B.-P. did not play cricket with Eloff but he did entertain him to dinner (such as it was) a few days later when Eloff was captured with sixty-eight other Boers endeavouring to storm into Mafeking by way of the River Molopo.

In all, the Mafeking defenders scored 217 days, not out. On the evening of May 16th, after dark, a messenger reached Mafeking to report that the relief force was encamped five miles outside the town and would enter in the morning. That night, for the first time for seven months, B.-P. went to bed with a quiet mind. He was wakened in the small hours of May 17th by someone shaking him by the shoulder; it was his brother, Baden, Intelligence Officer of the Relief Force, to say that Colonels Mahon and Plumer had arrived.

B.-P. had carried out the orders given him by Lord Wolseley. He had raised his two regiments; through Colonel Plumer he had defended the Rhodesian and Bechuanaland frontiers; but, more than both of these, through defending a small and relatively unimportant town in the middle of the veldt, he had kept thousands of the Boers' best troops pinned down for seven months 'away from their own forces'. That was the significance of the Defence of Mafeking. That, and the fact that it kept up British spirits at home during a period of shaky confidence. The cheeky and dogged defence had made B.-P. a hero to every Englishman and now Queen Victoria made him a Major-General — at forty-three the youngest in the British Army. It was the pinnacle of his career as a soldier.

Yet, looking back over his career in the army, it becomes clear that, paradoxically, he was not a man of war. He was happiest when he was scouting. When he did fight, he fought with courage and a flair for tactics, but he and the enemy fought with mutual respect and, at times, even with liking. The Boer War was really the last of the 'gentlemanly' wars. In

later life, B.-P. was to criticise the use of indiscriminate bomb-
ing in warfare. He felt that with its slaughter of civilians, it
gave rise to bitterness that would fester into hatred.

The war was not yet over. It dragged on for another two
years of fierce guerrilla fighting and cost Britain 20,000 lives
before peace was finally agreed in May of 1902 and the Boers
became British subjects. But Cecil Rhodes was right. 'You
think you have beaten the Dutch!' he said. 'It is not so. The
Dutch are not beaten. What is beaten is Krugerism, a corrupt
and evil government, no more Dutch in essence than English.
No! The Dutch are as vigorous and unconquered today as they
have ever been; the country is still as much theirs as yours, and
you will have to live and work with them hereafter as in the
past.'

It was strange that B.-P., who had contributed in some
measure to that so-called 'defeat' was to become so soon the
creator of the 'working and living together' that Rhodes envisaged — and not just between Dutch and English but between
boys of every race and creed.

CHAPTER 10

'. . . A Modern Major-General'

THERE WAS STILL work for B.-P. in South Africa. First of all, he was given command of a large area of the Transvaal with a view to rounding up Boer commandos, installing magistrates to restore order, and subduing bands of natives who had taken the opportunity of the white men's quarrels to plunder abandoned Boer farms. Occasionally he had a foretaste of the adulation that he was to have to face when he returned to England and that was to surround him for the rest of his life. He was staggered by the reception he had in Pretoria:

'It was awfully embarrassing,' he wrote home to his mother. 'I felt as if I were the Queen — and didn't know whether to grin or bear it — so did both.'

Before leaving Pretoria, B.-P. was interviewed by the war correspondent of the London *Morning Post*. The young man had bounced up again as he had promised he would two years before: it was Winston Churchill once more.

At the end of August, B.-P. received instructions from Lord Roberts to form a Police Force for the Transvaal, Orange River Colony and Swaziland. It was felt imperative that order should be restored throughout the country as soon as possible. Lord Roberts, in recommending B.-P. for the task of putting this in hand, had written: 'Baden-Powell is far and away the best man I know. He possesses . . . energy, organisation, knowledge of the country, and a power of getting on with its people.'

Thus the South African Constabulary came officially into being, with B.-P. as its Inspector-General. It was 'to act as a police force in and throughout the Transvaal and Orange River Colony for preserving the peace; and also as a military force for the defence of the Colonies.' All this was to be completed by June 1901.

It was a job after B.-P.'s heart — but it was not as simple as at first appeared. For one thing, the 'mopping up' operations were proving more prolonged and difficult than had been anticipated and the only officers, therefore, who could be spared from the Army to the S.A.C. were the 'cast-offs' who had been responsible for what were termed 'regrettable incidents' in the various campaigns. B.-P. took the view that men who had made mistakes were not likely to repeat them in the future and took them on. His trust in them was not disappointed. He established recruiting offices in Cape Colony and Natal and 'raked in men and officers wherever we could get them from all over the Empire'.

There was equipment to acquire, and buildings, and horses, and veterinary equipment — and uniform. This B.-P. designed himself. Remembering how much he himself enjoyed the 'flannel-shirt life', he introduced the informal khaki shirt and broad-brimmed hat that had, time and again, proved so comfortable for travelling around the veldt.

In a number of aspects, the South African Constabulary proved to have been a 'dry run' for Scouting, even to the slogan the men themselves chose: 'Be Prepared'.

By the end of June, 1901, B.-P. had by phenomenal effort and hard work almost built up and trained his force to the 10,000 men required — but at a cost to his own health. He was utterly exhausted with all this effort coming on top of the seven months' privation of the Mafeking siege. He collapsed and was firmly ordered back to England for six months' sick leave.

His reception at home was overwhelming. Everyone seemed to want to shower him with honours. There were civic receptions; Charterhouse asked him to lay the foundation stone of their Memorial Cloister; Australia sent him a gold-mounted Sword of Honour. There were sacks and sacks of mail awaiting him — and his new sovereign, King Edward VII, invited him to Balmoral and created him a Companion of the Order of the Bath. The King also gave him a walking stick and a haunch of venison to take home with him. 'I have watched you at meals and notice you don't eat enough,' said the King. 'When working as you are doing, you must keep up your system. Don't forget — eat more!'

It was on this occasion also that the King, whose powers of

observation made him a man after B.-P.'s own heart, observed: 'I suppose this is the first opportunity since your promotion to General that you've had an occasion to wear full-dress uniform. Are those spurs real gold or gilt?'

And B.-P. had to admit that they were, indeed, real gold — a gift from the people of Lewisham.

But even as the minister was praising the work of the S.A.C. and outlining its prospects for the future, events were moving towards yet another promotion for B.-P. He was offered the appointment of Inspector-General of Cavalry for Great Britain and Ireland, the Blue Riband of the Cavalry Service.

Once again he returned to a new address in London. 8 St. George's Place had been demolished to make way for Hyde Park Corner Station on the 'Tuppenny Tube' and Mrs. Baden-Powell and her daughter Agnes were now installed at 32 Princes Gate, S. W. 7.

It was an interesting time to take on the top job in cavalry for the Boer War had taught a number of lessons about the use of horses in warfare. That untrained Boers could, time after time, out-ride and out-manoeuvre trained cavalrymen indicated that there was something wrong with the British Army's ideas about cavalry training. B.-P. had been brought up in the tradition of the dramatic cavalry charge but had seen in Africa of how little use was such an exercise. He decided to study the techniques of other countries.

He visited America where, during the Civil War, use had been made of highly mobile cavalry units for scouting. He went to Canada to talk to the military leaders there. He visited the French Cavalry School at Saumur. He went, not as in 1886 as an amateur spy, but this time as an official observer to the German Army manoeuvres outside Dresden. The Kaiser treated him with genial courtesy and asked him his opinion of the Uhlans' lances.

'Too long to be practical,' was B.-P.'s comment.

'But where could you have *practical* experience with a lance?' asked the Emperor.

'You could always try pig-sticking, sire,' replied B.-P.

As a result of his observations, he was able to make practical recommendations for the improvement of cavalry training in the British Army of which one of the most notable was the foundation of a Cavalry College to train officers in equitation. Moreover, that training, he insisted, should take the form of *horsemanship* — creating a team of man and beast — not 'breaking in' the two by rigid drills. So many of his innovations are accepted practice today that it is easy to forget how far in advance of his times was his thinking. Just as in the Second World War, Field-Marshal Montgomery said 'One man can lose me a battle,' so B.-P. insisted that a chain of responsibility from the highest officer right down to the ranks would increase efficiency.

He was always one to know his men. His inspections of cavalry units were no longer the 'spit and polish' parades of former times; he preferred to spend several days with a unit, to watch the men and horses under working conditions, to talk to the younger officers as well as the senior ones and to draw out their ideas and enthusiasms.

By the time his tour of duty as Inspector-General of Cavalry came to an end on May 5th, 1907, B.-P. was already experimenting with the ideas that developed into the Boy Scout Movement but he could not guess at that time that a whole new life was opening up before him.

He was promoted Lieutenant-General on June 10th, 1907 but at the moment there was no job for him. As far as the Army was concerned, he was, though still a serving officer, no longer on the active list. Therefore, even though he was a general, he was on half-pay.

CHAPTER 11

An Experiment of Consequence

THE SCOUT MOVEMENT is today so much an accepted part of the social scene both in Britain and throughout the world that it is in danger of becoming considered an institution. It is difficult to imagine a time when Scouting did not exist and even more difficult to visualise what a complete innovation were its methods and ideals.

B.-P. did not consciously set out to found a new movement for boys. In a way, like Topsy in *Uncle Tom's Cabin*, it 'just grow'd'.

Whether he liked it or not, the gallant defence of Mafeking had turned B.-P. into a hero. His gaily inventive exploits fired the imagination of young people wherever his story was known. Moreover, his *Aids to Scouting* had become a best-seller. Widely read by old and young alike, long before he arrived back in England to take up his cavalry appointment, he began to receive letters from boys in all walks of life. They wrote to tell him how much they admired him; they wrote to ask his advice. Whereas many men would either have sent a formal acknowledgment or would have dropped the letters in the waste-paper basket after reading them, B.-P. took pains over answering each one. It was a practice he was to continue all his life. Just as he had made time for every man in the small family of his regiment, now he made time for an ever-increasing family of boys around the world.

His was always a positive approach. 'You should not be content with sitting down to defend yourselves against evil habits,' he wrote in reply to a letter from a Boys' Club, 'but should be active in doing good.' Here was the adult version of the eight-

Scouting was the link that tied B.-P.'s two lives together

year-old Stephe who had concluded his *Laws for Me When I am Old* with the sentence: 'You must pray to God whenever you can, but you cannot be good with only praying.' It was a child's version of St. James's 'faith without works is dead.'

When B.-P. returned to London in the Spring of 1903, it was not just to a new home but to see a transformed society. Except for an occasional short leave, he had been out of the country for eight years and he was dismayed to see the extent of the trade depression and unemployment that had followed the Boer War, the general decline in standards and, in particular, the apathy of so many young people — 'thousands of boys and young men pale, narrow-chested, hunched-up, miserable specimens, smoking endless cigarettes, numbers of them betting'.

It was not surprising, then, that when in May 1903 he was invited to attend the annual demonstration of Sir William Smith's Boys' Brigade in the Albert Hall, he was impressed by their smartness and discipline. The Coming-of-Age Review of the Brigade which he inspected the following year in Glasgow impressed him equally. There were seven thousand youngsters on parade, out of a membership of some 54,000. B.-P. congratulated Sir William on the turn-out. He was, however, somewhat concerned that the programme of the Brigade seemed to be largely a copy of the old-fashioned military drill of the army. If the programme of training were more varied, he suggested, Sir William would have four times as many recruits.

He asked how I would add to its attraction [B.-P. wrote some years later] and I told him how scouting had proved its popularity with young men in the cavalry, and that something of that kind might prove equally attractive to these younger boys, while its aim might easily be diverted from war to peace, since the inculcation of character, health and manliness was its basis, and these qualities were as much needed in a citizen as in a soldier. He cordially agreed with my idea and suggested that I should write a book for boys on the lines of *Aids to Scouting*.

Thus, in the odd moments he had to spare from his duties as Inspector-General of Cavalry, B.-P. had begun to jot down ideas.

It was no good writing the sort of book that sounded patronising, that said in so many words: 'If you read this you will become a useful citizen.' The book would have to be interesting in its own right. He knew too well — from his long experience of training soldiers, from his experience of spying and reconnaissance, from recollections of his own adventurous trips as a boy with his brothers, from memories of stalking in the woods around Charterhouse — that whatever programme he presented must be practical, must be adventurous, must be *fun*. B.-P. took boys seriously; he never talked down to them. He knew instinctively that, if you set them a challenge, they would rise to meet it.

He wanted a scheme that would inculcate habits of self-reliance and concern for others. He wanted to effect this by developing powers of observation and reasoning, by teaching practical skills and encouraging physical fitness, by instilling the virtues of self-discipline and obedience. Above all, it must be based on things *boys liked to do*, that would capture their imagination. But how best to do it?

He mulled the problem over in his mind for two years and not until April 1906 did he manage to sketch out some programme suggestions which, under the title *Scouting for Boys*, he sent to Sir William Smith. *The Boys' Brigade Gazette* in reviewing the scheme was polite but not very enthusiastic. There was too much emphasis on doing activities as a small group or gang rather than in company formation.

Hearing that his *Aids to Scouting* was being used in some schools, B.-P. looked at it again but decided it could not really be revised to suit peacetime conditions and boys. It would be much better to write a new book altogether. With his usual thoroughness, he read and studied everything he could lay hands on concerning the training of young men both past and present, from Livy, the Roman historian, to the Swiss educational reformer, Pestalozzi; from Spartans and Zulus to the Code of Chivalry of the knights of old. He examined the structure of all the existing youth organisations. He talked to friends such as Lord Roberts, to officials of the Y.M.C.A. and, with great interest and profit, to the writer Ernest Thompson Seton who had made a study of the American Indian and his woodcraft. He kept remembering Lord Edward Cecil's cadets at Mafeking, the way in which they were organised and the surprising ease with which they had assumed responsibility. The outcome of his research was circulated in the form of two four-page pamphlets which he sent to people who might be interested. One was entitled *Boy Scouts, A Suggestion*; the other *Boy Scouts, Summary of Scheme*. These outlined the object, reasons and methods of B.-P.'s scheme, the subjects to be taught, the games to be used, and suggested that an 'inexpensive and illustrated handbook, *Scouting for Boys*, should accompany the scheme.

One paragraph is particularly noteworthy in that it shows that it was not really in B.-P.'s mind to start a new youth *organisation*, though he could foresee that some such idea might be acceptable to boys not already attached:

It [the scheme] is intended to be applicable — and not in opposition — to any *existing* organisation for boys, such as schools, boys' brigades, messengers, cricket clubs, cadet corps, etc. or it can supply an organisation of its own where these do not exist — for there are one and three-quarter million boys in the country at present outside the range of these good influences, mostly drifting towards hooliganism for want of a helping hand.

One question B.-P. always asked of any scheme was 'Will it work?' He decided to try out his 'Boy Scout' scheme on real boys. Remembering his own joy in the 'flannel-shirt life' and bearing in mind that the countryside has so much to offer people who have been surrounded all their lives by bricks and mortar, he decided to have a camp in the country at which his ideas would be tested. The boys should be chosen from varying social backgrounds; he felt that sons of wealthy parents needed the training of a scout quite as much as the poor. In this B.-P. ignored the strict class-consciousness which still existed at the beginning of the century. Boys were what mattered; not the homes they came from.

B.-P.'s experimental camp on Brownsea Island off Poole in Dorset in August 1907 was to prove only the first of millions of Scout camps that have been held since all over the world. There were twenty-two boys in all under canvas — twenty-one from varied backgrounds ranging from working-class to public school. The twenty-second was B.-P.'s nine-year-old nephew Donald whom his brother George's widow persuaded him to take along as 'orderly'. B.-P.'s old friend from Indian and African days, 'The Boy' McLaren, made up the party.

Rations and equipment had to be ferried across to the island from Poole and the local Boys' Brigade undertook to do this — though some items of equipment B.-P. demanded were 'not readily obtainable in a small seaside town' — harpoons, for instance! Those had to be made by the local blacksmith.

What a thrill that first camp must have been! Just to be living alongside the Hero of Mafeking would have been excitement enough, but to see the actual flag that flew over his H.Q. in the besieged town now fluttering from a lance-point outside his tent was romance indeed. To be roused each morning by a deep blast on the koodoo horn he had brought back from the Matabele campaign! To spend the days in woodcraft and scouting exercises, to spend the evenings gathered round a camp-fire listening to the yarns that B.-P. told of faraway places where he had served! To join together in prayer under the summer stars and then to turn in to listen to the unfamiliar sounds of the night, and to sleep the contented sleep that comes with fresh air and exercise and happiness!

The boys learned to make the calls of their patrols. The cry of the curlew was heard along the shores of Brownsea Island and bulls bellowed even in its woods. There was cooking over open fires, 'harpooning' of log 'whales' on the island's lake, stalking of each other *and* visitors to the island. B.-P. remembered John Dunn's Zulu *impi* and the impression the deep-throated chant of the warriors had made on him. He even remembered the words and the translation John Dunn had given him. He taught the chant to those first Scouts and shrill young voices sought to emulate the deep-throated chant of the Zulus:

> Eengonyama Gonyama! Invooboo!
> Ya-boh! Ya-boh! Invooboo!
>
> He is a lion. Yes, he is better than a lion!
> He is a hippopotamus!

After the ten-day camp, B.-P. hurried back to London and arranged for the circulation of his third pamphlet: *Boy Scouts, A Successful Trial.*

Perhaps he was a little premature — the Brownsea Island Camp had cost him £55 2s. 6d. The amount received in camp fees (3s. 6d. per head!) and donations had only amounted to £30 11s. 6d. The Brownsea Island Experimental Camp had made a loss of £24 11s. 2d.

But it had shown that the idea did work. All that remained now was to get down to writing the handbook.

CHAPTER 12

'Scouting for Boys'

B.-P. HAD CONSIDERED in turn the various firms that had published his previous books but none of them had seemed right for *Scouting for Boys*. He needed one which would produce a cheap handbook and which would give full publicity to the scheme so that it could reach as many boys as possible. He met the publisher Arthur Pearson at a country house weekend in July and, inevitably, B.-P.'s projected scheme came up for discussion. Before he left for the Brownsea experiment, B.-P. had promised a rough draft of the book and a scheme had been planned whereby it would be printed in several parts by Horace Cox and would be distributed throughout the country on Pearsons' bookstalls. It was also decided that Pearsons would publish an exciting weekly paper for boys through which B.-P. could answer questions and develop ideas.

B.-P. had borrowed the use of a friend's cottage adjoining the famous windmill on Wimbledon Common in order to be undisturbed and had managed to complete his first draft of the book the week before he left for camp. He entered into a contract with Pearsons. They would publish the book and the paper and would contribute £1,000 to any expenses which might ensue, such as the running of an office to deal with enquiries. Any proceeds from the book would be used to finance the running of the 'scheme'. B.-P. insisted that the contract only run for a year; he did not want to be everlastingly tied to Pearsons. The writing of the book was not going to be easy to fit in if there was to be a weekly paper as well. Moreover, Pearsons insisted as a further term of the contract that B.-P. agree to undertake a lecture tour to explain the Boy Scout scheme. Now came a further difficulty.

Even Lieutenant-Generals, provided they are still serving officers, have to obtain permission from the army authorities before they can have anything published and before they can take on other jobs. All B.-P.'s previous books had been concerned with aspects of his work in the Army so there had been no problems. *Scouting for Boys* was going to be a different kind of book altogether. On September 1st, 1907 B.-P. sent a copy of his circular on *Boy Scouts* to R. B. Haldane, the Secretary of State for War, asking 'whether there was any likelihood of the Army wanting my services shortly and so interrupting me in the starting of the Scouts'.

In reply, Haldane invited B.-P. to his home in Scotland. He was himself working on a new project which, if it was approved, would require B.-P. to raise and train a force of 40,000 men to form the nucleus of a new 'Territorial Army' of volunteers in case of war. Haldane had no objection to the Scouting scheme provided it did not clash with his own. In the event, B.-P. was just able to fulfil his contract with Pearsons because the *Territorial and Reserve Forces Act* was not passed by Parliament for another two months and B.-P. was not required to take up his new command until April 1st, 1908. He would have a few months in hand. During intervals in his lecture tour which took him all over the country, he borrowed the peace of the Wimbledon Mill House again and, by dint of very hard work, managed to deliver the manuscript of each instalment in his book just one jump ahead of the printer!

B.-P. had to some extent prepared the ground with his lectures but the harvest that grew from that soil exceeded his wildest expectations.

Part I of *Scouting for Boys* appeared on Wednesday, January 15th, 1908, price 4d. The artist who designed the cover, John Hassall, had done a marvellous job to attract potential readers. There was no mistaking the author for a start. The magic words 'by B.-P.' were in larger type even than the title. And the drawing on the jacket was exciting: a boy lies behind a rock overlooking the seashore. Away at the water's edge is a small boat from which a party is landing. Smugglers? Enemy invaders? Further out at sea is a ship. Enemy? British warship to the rescue? Customs vessel? Any number of interpretations could be made. Beside the boy lie a staff and a broad-brimmed wideawake hat such as B.-P. had worn in Africa.

The books sold out as soon as they appeared on the bookstalls. Indeed, *Scouting for Boys* ranks third after the Bible and Shakespeare among the world's 'best-sellers'. Even at the (for

T–D

Part I.

Price 4d. n

SCOUTING FOR BOYS

BY B-P

LIEUT. GEN.
BADEN POWELL C.

PUBLISHED BY HORACE COX,
WINDSOR HOUSE, BREAM'S BUILDINGS, LONDON E.C

The original cover of *Scouting For Boys*, by John Hassall

1908) high price of 4d., the books were good value. Here were no stuffy lectures on moral precepts but instead a series of 'Camp-Fire Yarns' full of the things boys love to read about: detective yarns, adventure stories, tales of high chivalry. Mixed up among them were suggestions of activities that promised adventure out-of-doors, that challenged the reader's sense of honour, that spurred him to chivalrous pursuits. Without realising it, he was taking in B.-P.'s own high standards of reverence for God and His creation, of practical expression of that reverence in help for other people, in his insistence on practical skills and self-reliance.

It is not difficult to work out the genesis of his ideas and ideals from his own experience. Take, for example, the ten points of the Scout Law as they appeared in the original *Scouting for Boys*.

A Scout's honour is to be trusted. Time and again during his career, B.-P. had proved that discipline needs to come from within. It cannot be imposed by orders and regulations. Whether it was a request to his regiment in India not to frequent the bazaars in an attempt to check the spread of enteric fever; or whether it was giving failed officers a second chance in the South African Constabulary, B.-P. found that trust produced better results than orders.

A Scout is loyal to the King, his country, his Scouters, his parents, his employers and to those under him. B.-P. saw no cause for shame in honest patriotism, particularly when that included respecting the laws of his country and maintaining a decent standard of behaviour. All through his life, too, he loyally looked after his mother's interests, obeyed his Commanding Officers and cared for the men in his charge.

A Scout's duty is to be useful and to help others. He had grown up in a Christian household where consideration for other people, whether they be family or neighbours or strangers, was the accepted order of the day. In the army he had put this into practice by being always available to his men, ready to listen to their problems and to give practical help wherever he could.

A Scout is a friend to all, and a brother to every other Scout no matter to what country, class or creed the other may belong. Dangers shared with Zulu scouts, talks in Pretoria with young Afrikanders, hospitality from Boer farmers, Cecil Rhodes's vision of a united South Africa — all these had contributed to

B.-P.'s own vision of a world-brotherhood of Scouts.

A Scout is courteous. Here was some of his uncle's influence. Sir Henry Smyth had schooled his nephew well not only in the social graces required of an A.D.C. but, more important in the patience that is at the heart of true courtesy. Without courtesy, B.-P. could never have kept control of the civilian population of Mafeking during the siege, could not have written the polite notes that earned him the respect of the enemy commanders.

A Scout is a friend to animals. The boy who loved to watch the wild life of the woods round Charterhouse grew into the Inspector-General of Cavalry who insisted on *horsemanship* rather than drill in cavalry training. It needed a genuine love of animals to transform a working hack into a first-class polo pony, or (in an age when big-game trophies were the accepted appointments of an officer's quarters) to resist the temptation to shoot elephants when they were sitting targets.

A Scout obeys orders of his parents, Patrol Leader or Scout-master without question. Discipline had been instilled into him from his earliest years, by Warington aboard the *Kohinoor*, by his career in the army. He recognised the need for a clear chain of command and the importance of leadership.

A Scout smiles and whistles under all difficulties. It was well known at Mafeking that when the Commander whistled 'Wait till the clouds roll by', he was concealing his anger! More than this, however, he early recognised that laughter is a wonderful healer. All those theatricals for bored troops in India and Malta, the improvised shows during the siege of Mafeking which eased tensions and fears — these showed that a confident and smiling aspect could put heart into the most demoralised people.

A Scout is thrifty. From his earliest years, B.-P. had had to 'make do'. There was never any money to spare. But in having to 'make do', he discovered in himself and used to the full talents which might otherwise have been neglected.

A Scout is clean in thought, word and deed. (This 'Law' was not in the original first fortnightly part of *Scouting for Boys* but was added later.) Keeping cholera and enteric fever at bay in India had demonstrated the importance of hygiene, but more than physical cleanliness was embodied in this last 'law'. He had been shocked by the loutish behaviour of much of the youth of the country when he returned home in 1903 and realised how demoralising and destructive such behaviour could be. And, of course, he had on occasion had to deal with the consequences of immoral behaviour on the part of the men under his command and knew what tragedies could result.

These were the 'Rules' of the game of Scouting. They were eagerly accepted by the new Scouts, along with the secret signs of the salute and the left handshake and the demanding Promise. As with the Mafeking Cadets, B.-P. recognised that no matter how high the standard set as a target, boys would strive to reach it.

Every other Wednesday until the end of March 1908 boys (and girls, too) eagerly awaited the next instalment of *Scouting for Boys*.

The idea of carrying out activities in small gangs or 'patrols' also had great appeal. It was an idea first tried out officially in the Ashanti campaign — though B.-P. probably recalled how well he worked with his older brothers in their small family 'gang'.

It was suggested that Scout 'patrols' could be formed within existing organisations but, somehow, they never did. Boys wanted to be *Scouts* — not Cadet-Scouts, or Brigade-Scouts, or School-Scouts or any other than B.-P. Scouts. Long before the sixth and final instalment had appeared on the bookstalls, Scout Patrols and Troops had sprung up like mushrooms up and down the British Isles. Without any warning, chalk tracking signs appeared on pavements, camp-fires smoked on suburban commons, hardware stores sold out of broom handles, knickerbockers were cut into shorts, and the elderly were overwhelmed with offers of assistance.

What was it about B.-P. and his book that brought boys thronging after him in their hundreds, their thousands and eventually in their millions? There was a promise of adventure, certainly. But there was more than that. B.-P. could make life with all its difficulties appear like a glorious game to be won, just as he had turned the Defence of Mafeking into a gallant game, too. He managed to tap the spring of idealism that is inherent in every boy.

He gave them a motto to which everyone could subscribe: 'Be Prepared'. He gave them ten Laws which were not gloomy prohibitions but had the positive appeal of 'A Scout *is* . . .' He gave them a Promise which, if faithfully observed, could keep a man true and God-loving for the whole of his life:

On my honour, I promise that I will *do my best*
To do my duty to God, and the King (Queen),
To help other people at all times,
And to obey the Scout Law.

How the idea of the daily 'Good Turn' caught the imagination both of the boys and of the general public! Such a simple idea, based on Jesus's command to 'love your neighbour'. Yet just as that simple-sounding command is so difficult of achievement, so the daily good turn called for self-discipline and unselfishness. Yet it became a matter of principle with every Scout not to fail in his Good Turn and many even went so far as to tie a knot in their tie, as B.-P. suggested, in order to remind themselves not to do just one good turn but to make consideration for others a way of life.

The numbers grew. The tiny office in Henrietta Street, London which Pearsons had set aside to deal with any enquiries, was swamped with mail. Boys wrote to ask where they could buy hats, tents, cooking-pots, whistles. There were letters from retired soldiers, from schoolmasters, from clergymen asking for more information about the Movement and its rules. Yet there was no 'Movement', there were no 'Rules' — yet.

A new weekly, *The Scout*, was rushed into print, with the same evocative cover as the first part of *Scouting for Boys*. It was well-edited, full of exciting stories and articles and it contained the first of more than 1,500 pieces that B.-P. himself was to contribute over the years. Within a short time, circulation had risen to 110,000 copies a week. Far from stemming the flow of letters to what were now inevitably known as 'Boy Scout Headquarters', the magazine only served to stimulate the flow; and enquiries were flooding in from all parts of the Empire.

In the midst of this, B.-P., had to go north to start creating Haldane's Territorial Army!

He had been given command of the Northumbrian Division, covering the territory between the Humber and the Scottish border, and it was accordingly necessary that he lived in the north for the time being. But *The Scout* had run a competition offering as a prize to the top thirty boys an opportunity to go to summer camp with B.-P. There could be no question of another Brownsea Island camp; his work with 'The Terriers' precluded that. So the camp would have to come north to him.

For ten days, the 'gallant thirty' camped at Humshaugh in Northumberland within sight of the Roman Wall. The weather was atrocious for much of the time but on this occasion it did not matter. Unlike Brownsea, on this occasion the Scouts had had some training.

Another camp was organised partly at Buckler's Hard, Beaulieu in Hampshire and partly on the training ship *Mercury*. The lads aboard the ship enjoyed it so much that it gave B.-P. the idea of founding Sea Scouts as well.

The whole thing was growing so big and so fast, B.-P. realised at last that he would have to bow to the inevitable and allow Scouting to be a Movement in its own right.

CHAPTER 13

Second Life

1909 WAS A crucial year in the development of Scouting for in that year the organisation of the Movement took on something of the shape that persists today. There were about 100,000 boys already enrolled as Scouts. B.-P. felt it was time to try out a suggestion that had been put forward by several people: to have a big gathering of Scouts from all over the country, preferably in London, to show the public what Scouting was all about. Hence the great Crystal Palace Rally of September 1909.

Inevitably, it was 'B-P. weather' — pouring rain! However, nothing could dampen the enthusiasm of the 11,000 Scouts who took part in the display. But when he toured the ranks of excited boys to inspect their work, he had a surprise. In one part of the arena he came upon a group of seven girls, all wearing Scout hats and scarves and carrying staves.

'Who are you?' asked B.-P.

'We are the Girl Scouts,' was the astounding reply.

That set him a problem. In those days, the activities of boys and girls were kept entirely separate. If he allowed girls into the Movement, the boys would declare that Scouting was 'sissy' and leave — and the girls' parents would in any event be outraged at what would at that time be considered immodest behaviour. But he recognised that something should be done for the girls; there was absolutely nothing for girls to do other than 'suitable' domestic activities.

> Dear Sir [one of them wrote] If a girl is not allowed to run, or even to hurry, to swim, ride a bike, or raise her arms above her head, can she become a Scout? Hoping that you will reply.
>
> Yours sincerely,
> A WOULD-BE SCOUT

The only thing was to start a new Movement for them also, with a programme drawn up on Scout lines but including activities more suited to young ladies. He therefore created the Girl Guides and persuaded his sister Agnes to be in charge — and this Movement, too, began to spread, though as yet not as swiftly as Scouting.

Inevitably, when anything new arrives, it has its critics. Scouting was no exception to this. Pacifists declared it was a militaristic plot to conscript boys for military training. The military-minded criticised the Movement for missing an opportunity for instilling 'a firm military spirit into the youth of the country' and instead dissipating its energies in children's games. Posters appeared in Ireland warning that 'the Baden-Powell Scouts are established in Dublin to tempt Irish boys to betray their country to be loyal to England's King.' One of the loudest criticisms, however, was that Scouting was not affiliated to any church as were all other youth organisations at that time. In vain did B.-P. explain that he had not planned a *new* Movement, only an adjunct to existing ones; that he *had* included 'Duty to God' as a requirement of all Scouts. Still the criticism continued.

The only thing to do was to gather together the leaders of all the major religious denominations and formulate a religious policy that was satisfactory to all. This was done in September 1909 and the policy has been kept under constant review ever since by the Religious Advisory Board at Scout Head-quarters.

Moreover, it became apparent as Scouting spread throughout the world and was embraced with enthusiasm by boys of other faiths than Christianity, that here was an opportunity to encourage those factors that are common to the religions of the world rather than harp on questions that divide them. In making the first requirement of the Scout Promise simply duty to *God*, Scouting was recognising that boys of other faiths were in their own way acknowledging the existence of a Supreme Being. Thus, through Scouting, boys of *all* faiths could join in brotherhood, each serving his own God but all seeking to serve their neighbours as emphasised in the second part of the Promise.

Of such problems, however, the proud new Scouts were oblivious. They had their own problems to face. It was hard if you were only eleven or twelve years old not to be a little scared when louts in their late 'teens pelted your new uniform with horse-dung and yelled at you:

> 'Here come the Brussels Sprouts,
> The stinking, blinking, bleeding louts . . .'

But you thought of what your hero, B.-P., might have done in such a situation, or one of King Arthur's knights, or the Indian brave whose signs and smoke signals you had learned about in last week's Yarn. And you straightened your thin shoulders and grasped your staff and turned to face the bullies . . .

King Edward VII watched the development of the new Movement with interest. Once again, B.-P. was invited to Balmoral and on this occasion was knighted.

'Just before dinner the King sent for me,' he wrote to his mother. 'The equerry . . . took me to his room and while outside the door took off my miniature medals . . . and ordered a footman to take in a cushion. It was very like preparation for an execution . . .'

When he went down to dinner after the ceremony, he found it strange to be addressed by his new title. 'I didn't realise at first who they were alluding to when they said "Sir Robert" does this or that.'

The King agreed to B.-P.'s request that boys who reached a certain very high standard of efficiency should be ranked as 'King's Scouts', and the King, in his turn, invited B.-P. to take his Scouts to Windsor the following year for a royal review.

It was becoming a struggle to keep pace with the growth of the Movement. Some decentralisation was needed and some delegation of responsibility — the policy B.-P. had so earnestly advocated in his schemes of Army training and in the South African Constabulary. There was no reason why it should not work just as well in Scouting although, B.-P. insisted, as it was a voluntary Movement, it should be governed by volunteers.

This was the thinking that led to the foundation of what is today the Council of the Association and its working executive, 'The Committee of the Council'. When the Boy Scouts Association was incorporated by Royal Charter in January 1912, the organisation had the final seal of approval set on it.

There was also the question of finance. To date, apart from the £1,000 Pearsons had put up in the beginning, the whole cost of running Scouting had come from the proceeds of the sale of

Scouting for Boys and the balance from B.-P.'s own pocket. This could not go on indefinitely, even with occasional donations from friends. So again, another sub-committee had to be set up to deal with the raising of funds but, as many of the volunteers on the Council were shrewd business men, B.-P. was able safely to leave that aspect of his worries in their hands.

His biggest remaining anxiety was how to cope with the demands of the Territorials as well as Scouting. He could no longer do both. It was an agonising decision to have to make for the army had been his whole life for over thirty years. Yet the Territorials were by now firmly established, whereas Scouting was spreading so fast that he needed all his energies to ensure that it developed everywhere along the right lines.

However, with the rank of general, the decision to resign from the Army was made easier; he had always preferred being a regimental officer in personal touch with his men. He discussed his plans with his friend, Lord Roberts, and with the Secretary of State for War. Haldane received his resignation with regret but wrote: 'I feel that this organisation of yours has so important a bearing on the future that probably the greatest service you can render to the country is to devote yourself to it.'

On May 5th, 1910, B.-P. went to Buckingham Palace. It was usual for a retiring general to pay his respects to his King — and in addition B.-P. wanted to discuss final details for the review of Scouts at Windsor that had tentatively been fixed for June.

When he arrived for his audience, an equerry told him that the King was not well but wanted to assure him that all was in order for the June review. He would see B.-P. when he felt better.

Two days later, on the same day that B.-P. officially retired, King Edward VII died.

CHAPTER 14

Double Harness

B.-P. WAS FIFTY-THREE when he retired from the Army and he was still unmarried. There had been plenty of opportunities. Many attractive girls in the past had set their caps at the young Hussar officer but he seemed wedded to his Army career. Moreover, though he was separated for years at a time from his mother, Mrs. Baden-Powell's hold over her sons was very strong. She had made it plain that she would consider it selfish if any of them were to marry and it was no doubt with great reluctance that she had had to accept first George's and then Frank's escape from her tight family circle.

B.-P. used to chaff his officers when, during service abroad, they eagerly looked for letters from their wives. 'Just you wait,' Major Gordon had warned him as long ago as the Ashanti campaign of 1895. 'You'll get it in the neck one day when you least expect it.'

As prophesied, he was quite unprepared when that day came upon him.

In four years, Scouting had not only swept like wildfire throughout the British Isles; it had spread round the world as well. There were Scouts all over Europe, in the United States and Canada, in Chile, in Australia, New Zealand and South Africa. Sooner or later, he would have to visit them.

In January 1912, he set off from Southampton aboard the *Arcadian* on the first leg of a world tour. The *Arcadian* was making a leisurely winter cruise to the West Indies and back. The first day out, B.-P. noticed two young ladies on deck. One of them he already knew; the other seemed vaguely familiar but he could not place her. The friend introduced them.

'You live in London,' said B.-P.

'No, in Dorsetshire,' she replied. Yet B.-P. was sure he knew her.

'But you have a dog — a brown and white spaniel,' he insisted.

The young lady was amazed. 'Yes, I have.'

'And you *have* been in London — near Knightsbridge Barracks?'

'Yes, I spent several months at Rutland Gate two years ago.'

B.-P.'s memory and observation were not at fault. He was always interested in the way people walked and, indeed, had included a paragraph on this subject in his 'Camp Fire Yarn No. 11' under the title *Observation and Deduction*. Two years earlier, he had noticed this particular young lady exercising her dog in Hyde Park and had decided that her firm step 'showed her to be possessed of honesty of purpose and common sense, as well as of the spirit of adventure.'

The young lady was Miss Olave Soames, cruising with her father, a wealthy landed gentleman who liked to winter away from England. B.-P. and Olave fell instantly and wildly in love and by the end of the six-week voyage were secretly engaged. They had to be circumspect for B.-P. was a public figure and Olave young enough to be his daughter. They did not dare to reveal their affection for each other in public because it would have outraged many people to see a fifty-five-year-old general apparently 'flirting' with a girl thirty-two years his junior. That was how the public would see it, even though their love was genuine and even though to B.-P., brought up in a family where there was a difference of twenty-eight years between his parents, there did not seem anything strange in such an age difference. They parted in Jamaica, Olave to return to England on the *Arcadian* and B.-P. to continue his world tour.

The courtship continued by letter and at one time seemed in danger of ending completely when B.-P.'s mother demanded that he put more of his pension into the communal fund as his brother Frank was ill and unable to contribute as much as before. B.-P. was in despair. He had not enough 'even to keep a dog', he wrote. How could he expect Olave to give up her luxurious home to live on his modest income? Olave brushed aside all difficulties. Thanks to her father's generosity, she would have enough for both of them. They were reunited at the end of August, married in October of 1912 and, as B.-P. in his autobiography summarised thirty years of married life, 'lived happily ever after'.

It turned out that B.-P. had acquired not just a wife but a wonderful partner in his work. Up to the time of her marriage, Olave had lived a very sheltered and, as she describes it, 'futile' existence as the youngest child of a very rich man. She had never done any kind of public work whatsoever. Something about B.-P. was to draw out the best in her as it had so surely done in many a soldier or Scout. She threw herself ardently into his work, which was a surprise and joy to those members of the Scout Movement who had wondered whether marriage would mean their beloved 'Chief' would give up Scouting. One small Scout had even gone so far as to write:

> I am dreadfully disappointed in you. I have often thought to myself 'How glad I am that the Chief Scout is not married, because if he was he could never do all these ripping things for boys.' And now you are going to do it. It is the last thing I should have expected of you. Of course, you won't be able to keep on with the Scouts the same as before, because your wife will want you, and everything will fall through. I think it is awfully selfish of you.

'The ripping things' were all too soon to change in character with the outbreak of war in August 1914 — a war that was going to test the foundation work B.-P. had put into the organisation of the Territorial Army and that was to show the nation just how splendidly his Boy Scouts could rise to the call of duty.

B.-P. had been proud, in December 1911, to be gazetted Colonel-in-Chief of his old regiment, the 13th Hussars, and on the outbreak of war immediately saw Lord Kitchener, now Secretary of State for War, and asked to be recalled for active service. But Kitchener knew that B.-P. could do more for his country in tapping the loyalty and dedication of his Scouts than ever he could in the field. He told B.-P. that he could think of no task more important at the present than for him to carry on with his work among young people. 'We have several good generals,' he said 'but no one who could carry on with the invaluable work of the Boy Scouts.' 'So I came home very bucked!' B.-P. wrote in his diary.

He threw himself tirelessly into organising their war work.

The Scouts guarded bridges and telegraph lines against possible sabotage; they acted as messengers in Government Departments, as orderlies in hospitals; assisted the Police; helped to get in the harvest. But perhaps their finest work was their night and day watch of the coast, right round Britain, which they carried out all through the war. 'Men of the Second Line', B.-P. called them.

In addition to his work with the Scouts, B.-P. was backwards and forwards to France, visiting his regiment in the line and also organising the setting up of recreation huts for the troops along the lines of the Y.M.C.A. huts. He was a member of the ancient livery company of the Mercers and was able to persuade them to finance the huts while arranging for Scout volunteers to man them.

Olave was unable at first to share in his war work for she was tied with two babies: Peter, born in 1913, and Heather, born in 1915. However, her mother agreed to look after the two children and Olave was able to go to France towards the end of 1915 to join her husband and to work for three months in the canteen of one of the huts.

B.-P.'s reputation and the publication in 1915 of his account of his early adventures under the title of *My Adventures as a Spy* naturally made his frequent visits to France seem suspicious to the enemy. There were rumours that he was Britain's Master Spy moving secretly in and out of Germany. One newspaper reported that he had been surprised in Berlin entering the German War Office disguised as a chimney-sweep! Another strong rumour had him escaping across the Baltic to Sweden and being brought out by destroyer. No doubt British Intelligence happily fostered these rumours.

His mother died in October 1914 at the great age of ninety, alert in mind to the last and proud to have held in her arms the firstborn of her distinguished son. It was a sad blow for B.-P. He often used to say that 'the whole secret of my getting on lay with my mother' — but it was to be only one loss among many as the war claimed more and more of his army colleagues and some 10,000 of his friends in Scouting.

As the first year of the war dragged on with mounting casualties and failure, the Guides had become restless to be of as much service as the Scouts. They had never really 'got off the ground' under his sister Agnes' leadership; she was far too Victorian in her outlook to keep pace with the swiftly moving times. And although she was a woman of immense talent, she had not her brother's imagination or ability to draw the best out of the members of her Movement. Indeed, Agnes had almost agreed that the Guides should be taken over by the much more dynamic Y.W.C.A.

Something had to be done — and quickly. In September 1915, thanks to B.-P.'s persistence, the Girl Guides Association was granted a Charter of Incorporation which made it an officially recognised body, secure from 'takeover'. At the same time, B.-P. made himself Chairman (transferring Agnes to the less active role of President) and set up a new, young Committee to run the Association. His wife had already, in 1914, offered her services to Guiding but on that occasion had been turned down! Now, under the new 'management' she became County Commissioner for Sussex and showed such energy and such a talent for organisation that she was elected in rapid succession Chief Commissioner (1916) and in February 1918, Chief Guide.

The Baden-Powell's third and last child, Betty, had been born in 1917 so, as the dreadful war finally drew to its close in November 1918, the two Chiefs were free to start together their peacetime work for the boys and girls of the world.

First of all, they had to find a home. Up to now, they had been in rented accommodation in various parts of Surrey and Sussex. Now that peace had come and their family had grown, it seemed a suitable time to put down roots.

The day after Armistice Day, they put their bicycles on the train to Farnham and went house-hunting. The Hampshire/Surrey border was far enough from town to give them the country atmosphere they both loved but was near enough to London for them to be able to get in quickly and easily to their respective Headquarters. Quite by accident, they happened on Blackacre Farm at Bentley which was exactly what they were seeking.

With help from Olave's generous father, they bought the house and eight acres of land, and moved in. They re-named the place 'Pax Hill' in honour of the peace that had at last come to war-torn Europe. It was to prove a Hill of Peace for over twenty years, not only for B.-P. and Olave and their family, but for all the thousands of visitors who came there over that period from all quarters of the globe to find inspiration and friendship in the company of this dynamic, talented and warm-hearted couple.

CHAPTER 15

Golden Years

IT WOULD BE a mammoth task to describe all the manifold activities of the Chief Scout during the remainder of his life. The highlights alone make up an impressive total.

Pessimists had declared that the war would 'kill' Scouting but it had not only proved its worth during that testing time but had emerged stronger than ever. In 1916, in response to the clamour of younger brothers for inclusion in the scheme, the Wolf Cub section had been formed for boys between eight and eleven. Now after the war, it became apparent that there was as much, if not a greater need for young men of goodwill and high standards to try to win the peace. This resulted in the Rover Scout section for young men of seventeen and over. Its programme concentrated on service to the community and to the Movement. Young men were growing up in a world full of new problems and pressures, and B.-P. was anxious that each of his Scouts should grow into a mature, well-balanced individual able to face up to these new pressures. He was proud that so many of Rover Scout age turned to him for advice about their problems and he dealt with each one individually and in confidence.

No one, he felt, was beyond the help of Scouting. 'It is far more satisfactory to turn one unruly character the right way than to deal with a dozen milk and water cases,' he had written in *Scouting for Boys*. Once again, the Christian principles on which he had based his life were applied to his Scouting. 'Suppose a man has a hundred sheep. If one of them strays, does he not leave the other ninety-nine on the hillside and go in search of the one that strayed?'

With the coming of peace, the Movement expanded even more and it became obvious that Scoutmasters themselves would need training if they were to give effective leadership. Once again, a genuine need received a prompt answer. A generous Scottish Scout Commissioner, W. de Bois Maclaren, purchased and presented to the Movement the derelict manor house and fifty-seven overgrown acres on the edge of Epping Forest in Essex that have been transformed over the years into the magnificent International Training Centre, Gilwell Park.

The first training course was held there in July 1919 and took somewhat the same form (though on an adult scale) as the first experimental camp at Brownsea Island. Once again the koodoo horn roused the camp, and it remains at Gilwell to this day. At the end of the course, the question arose as to what form of badge or certificate should be given to those Scoutmasters who had undertaken training. B.-P. remembered another trophy he had brought from Africa — Dinuzulu's necklace, the long rope of quaintly carved wooden beads he had found in the deserted fortress in the Ceza thirty years before. He decided to give each candidate one bead from the string to wear on a thong over the Scout scarf and this wooden bead gave its name to 'Wood Badge' training. When, after some years, the original long necklace ran out of beads, the Gilwell staff carved copies to keep up the tradition.

There have been many tales about B.-P.'s skill in interpreting tracks. He could read what he called a 'newspaper' in the snow, describing the humans and animals that had left their imprint. Capt. D. Penrose, who became an Assistant Scoutmaster in 1912, relates how he was on a training course at Gilwell in about 1921. The Chief Scout was giving a group instruction, making-use of a smoothly raked sandpit. He would set problems which the course had to work out — who had crossed the sandpit; how long ago; were they walking, running or carrying anything; how tall were they, and so on. After a while he said 'Now you set me a problem' and disappeared out of sight while they laid the necessary tracks. Imagine their amazement when he not only solved the problem but also added to one man 'You set up that part over there', and to another 'You did that part'. He had observed the size and shape of each individual's shoes.

They were determined to try to catch him out so asked him to go away while they set up a second problem for him. This time, they got hold of a small Shetland pony that lived on the estate and, with great difficulty, managed to *back* it across the sandpit. Then they returned it to its shed and called the Chief.

He studied the ground for a long minute, then looked up at them with eyes that were brimming with laughter. 'How *did* you manage to get him to do it?' he asked.

These tests were not mere 'parlour-tricks' but were designed to illustrate the importance of observation and deduction.

To signal the return of peace, it was decided to organise a great meeting of Scouts from all over the world that would demonstrate that the youth of all nations could indeed meet in brotherhood as B.-P. envisaged. The first World Jamboree was held at Olympia in London between July 30th and August 7th, 1920. At the concluding ceremony, the Movement took over from B.-P. For once, *he* was no longer in control as the representatives of twenty-seven nations invited him to be Chief Scout of the World.

That was only the first of many Jamborees that were to follow, once every four years, in different parts of the world — in places as far separated as Hungary and the Philippines, Canada and Japan. From the twenty-seven nations at Olympia, the number of countries who can now send representatives to a World Jamboree has grown to a hundred and fifty. Where else, except uneasily at the United Nations, do Jew and Arab sit down in peace together, Moslem with Hindu, black and brown and yellow and white-skinned boys meeting on equal terms? Princes sharing a camp with plumbers? Future kings with carpenters? Few men can have had a wider and more far-reaching influence for good throughout the world.

In his lifetime, B.-P.'s greatness was recognised in many ways, with honorary degrees from six universities, with 'freedoms' of great cities. Twenty foreign countries awarded him their highest honours. At home, King George V appreciated, no less than King Edward before him, that B.-P. was a man of vision dedicated to a great ideal. When the King created B.-P. a baronet in 1921, he was at first embarrassed at the honour until, as he wrote in his autobiography, 'I realised that it meant a mark of the King's appreciation of the voluntary work of this vast army of men who were devoting their time and energy and, in many cases, money to training boys to be better citizens for the country.'

Of the two honours, probably the title 'Chief Scout of the World' gave B.-P. the greater gratification.

However, the appointment brought with it responsibilities — to travel the world visiting all those Scouts who could never hope to attend a Jamboree, to meet their leaders, to watch always that Scouting (and Guiding too) was developing along the right lines.

He and Lady Baden-Powell had in 1920 made a 'whistle-stop' tour of the United States and Canada which had been a great success. They were to meet their first real challenge in international Scouting when in 1921 they were invited to India by the Viceroy, Lord Chelmsford, to sort out the muddled state of Scouting in that country. They found about six different unofficial Associations, all calling themselves Scouts but all in conflict one with another and some of them being even political in their bias! It took all B.-P.'s tact to persuade them to sink their differences and to unite together into one association that could be recognised officially by Headquarters.

The Viceroy was anxious that Scouting should be used as an adjunct to education in India. There were nearly ten million boys of Scout age in the country but many of them were lacking in any opportunity to learn about health or hygiene, quite apart from the moral principles and strengthening of character Scouting could offer.

There were already over a third of a million Scouts in India but this was only a fraction of the potential number. Even so, the difference of approach of these boys from non-Scouts was too outstanding to be dismissed as accident. For example, they helped to regulate the vast crowds at the *melas* or religious festivals; they had laboured with admirable courage on the rescue work following the Quetta earthquake. Actions like these, in a country where death and disaster are so often accepted as inevitable, denoted a marked improvement of attitude.

An example of the influence of Scouting on the day-to-day life of the community was shown in the changes that had taken place in a small village in Bombay Province. Conditions in the village were filthy, leading to constant outbreaks of illness. Nothing was ever done to improve matters because there was perpetual quarrelling between the three religious sects that made up the little community: the Jains, the Moslems and the Hindus.

One day a doctor arrived in the village who was also a Scouter. He gathered a few boys of all three sects around him, formed a Troop and taught all he knew of the principles of Scouting. Those first boys brought in other boys. As the numbers grew, the Scouts tried to help their own village. The street was cleared of refuse, a village centre was built; trees and flowers were planted. More than this, their happy spirit of service seemed to act as a leaven in the community and gradually the religious antagonisms became submerged in a desire to make the village a better and happier place for everyone to live.

It was an exciting tour. The Baden-Powells had a glowing reception wherever they went. They enjoyed the privilege of travelling in the Viceroy's personal train and saw something of the splendour of Viceregal Lodge in Delhi and the fabulous life-style of the Rajahs. In addition, B.-P. was delighted to show his wife the various places where he had been stationed during his years of army service in India. Though there were rumblings of the spirit of nationalism that was to lead to independence in 1947, much of India remained unchanged. There was still the challenge of the rigid caste system and of the appalling poverty arising so often out of ignorance — though it seemed that Scouting could do something towards breaking these things down.

There followed a succession of rallies and exhibitions: the 1922 'Posse of Welcome' for the then Prince of Wales (later, King Edward VIII) at Alexandra Palace; the Imperial Jamboree on the occasion of the British Empire Exhibition in 1924; visits to South Africa, the United States and Canada; trips to Denmark and Switzerland. In all of these, and more, B.-P. had the enthusiastic support of his wife. In between public occasions, they escaped to the quiet of Pax Hill where they could enjoy their children and entertain their friends.

Even there, B.-P. worked constantly. His output was phenomenal, even with the 'thirteenth' month that he managed to put into each year by beginning his day's work at five o'clock in the morning. During the twenty years he lived at Pax Hill and despite his advancing years, he produced a steady flow of books, articles, sketches and paintings which, even without any of his other commitments, would have been a considerable output in themselves.

Winter and summer, he slept outside on the balcony and every day performed the exercises he recommended to his Scouts, or walked for miles with his wife to exercise the dogs.

It was a wonderfully happy home, full of children and pets,

of riding-kit and fishing-tackle. Visitors were always welcome, whether it was an unexpected group who turned up to ask if they could camp in the grounds, or the entire staff of Scout Headquarters invited for a garden party; whether it was some dignitary from overseas or the young officers from the 13th Hussars stationed at Aldershot.

If there was one cloud over their happiness, it was that, having married so late in life, he might not survive to see his children grow up. On March 22nd, 1922, he wrote a birthday letter to his son that was to be opened seven years later; it was one of a numbered series he had prepared for Peter in the event of his death.

> My dear old Pete, I have just finished a very long letter to you for you to read when you are 16.
>
> It is my book *Rovering to Success*. It is mainly made up of things that I should like to have told you — but as they apply also to other boys growing to manhood I have published them for all to read.
>
> But I want you especially to read the book and be guided by it.
>
> It contains a lot of information and advice that I badly needed as a young man — but I had no father to give it to me. He died when I was 3.
>
> Your father will be dead, I expect, when you are 16 — but let that book help you in my place. Will you?
>
> Your loving,
>
> DAD

In the event, he was still very much alive when that letter was due to be opened. The year was 1929, the year of the great Coming-of-Age Jamboree in Arrow Park, Liverpool. That was the occasion when, very much against his wish, B.-P. became a peer of the realm. He felt that becoming a 'Baron' or 'Lord' might raise a barrier between himself and the boys he led. He liked always to feel that the Scouts viewed him as one of themselves, that they would not be shy of approaching him. However, he accepted the honour because his closest advisers persuaded him that he owed it to the Movement. His honour was an honour for all.

A much more welcome gift on that same day was a pair of

bright green braces — which he had said he particularly needed.
They were accompanied by a Rolls-Royce car (the 'Jam Roll'),
a trailer caravan (known as 'Eccles'), his portrait by David
Jagger and a handsome cheque. These wonderful gifts had been
purchased through each Scout in the *world* contributing one
penny towards the fund.

Becoming a peer entailed his taking his seat in the House of
Lords but he was never interested in politics. 'This world seems
divided into talkers and doers,' B.-P. once wrote to the students
at Edinburgh University. 'There are too many talkers. The
doer is the man we need — the man whose vision is not limited
by narrow party considerations.'

All his life, B.-P. was a 'doer' himself but as the twenties
moved into the thirties, he was less able to pursue the strenuous
programme he had achieved earlier. For a man in his seventies,
he set himself a punishing schedule. However, in 1930 Lady
Baden-Powell was chosen Chief Guide of the World and now,
wherever they travelled together, B.-P. was able to concentrate
on Scouting matters whereas before he had had to oversee
Guides as well.

They made a marvellous team when they went on a world
tour in 1931, concentrating in particular on Australia and New
Zealand which B.-P. had not visited since 1912. They had a
strenuous but exhilarating Scout and Guide Cruise to the
Baltic in 1933. It had been especially satisfying for B.-P. to see
the growth of Scouting in Poland, Lithuania, Latvia and Es-
tonia. Alas, these countries were soon to lose their freedom *and*
their Scouting, for Scouting belongs to the free world. There
had been Scouts in Russia when B.-P. had visited that country
in 1911 but they had disappeared after the 1917 Revolution,
suppressed by the Bolsheviks and kept suppressed by the Com-
munists who followed. In the same way, Scouts were suppressed in Italy and Germany when Mussolini and Hitler came
to power.

B.-P. met the Italian dictator in 1933 in Rome. Mussolini
was proud of the *Balilla*, his new organisation for boys. Were
they not definitely an improvement on Scouting, he boasted.
Not so, demurred B.-P. The *Balilla* were compulsory, not voluntary; they were fiercely nationalistic instead of international
in their outlook; most of all, their training was purely physical;
it completely disregarded the spiritual and moral training
which are needed to make the whole man.

Similarly, in November of 1937, an attempt was made by Baldur von Schirach, leader of the Hitler Youth, to establish some sort of liaison with Scouting but once again B.-P. knew that the essential elements of 'Duty to God' and brotherhood with other nations were missing.

As the clouds gathered over Europe and the world moved inevitably towards another and even more devastating war, so the Chief Scout also declined in health. The will and the imagination were as vigorous as ever but his strength was gradually failing. A serious illness early in 1934 brought the first realisation home to his Scouts that he could not go on for ever. He seemed always so young in spirit, so full of fun. It seemed as if he was indestructible.

He still, despite a serious operation, undertook yet another round-the-world voyage with Lady Baden-Powell during 1934–5, a further intensive tour of South Africa in 1936 and one to India at the beginning of 1937. But he knew he would not be able to carry on much longer.

The Fifth World Jamboree was held in Holland in the summer of 1937. His closing speech moved everyone who heard it; they guessed that he knew that he would not see another Jamboree:

> The time has come for me to say goodbye. You know that many of us will never meet again in this world. I am in my eighty-first year and am nearing the end of my life. Most of you are at the beginning . . .
>
> Now goodbye. God bless you all!

So many of them, indeed, would 'never meet again' for within two years the world was plunged into war. In Holland, where the Jamboree had been held, as in so many enemy-occupied countries, Scouts died heroically working in underground movements for the freedom of their countries. And once again, as in the 1914–1918 war, Scouts and Scouters the free world over threw themselves wholeheartedly into the fight against oppression.

CHAPTER 16

Gone Home

WHEN WORLD WAR II broke out in 1939, B.-P. was living in Kenya and was in his eighty-third year. It grieved him that he was too old to make any active contribution to the war effort.

Two years earlier, he and Lady Baden-Powell had stayed at the Outspan, a hotel at Nyeri founded and run by Eric Walker who had been Secretary of the Scout Association in its early days. They had loved the quiet peace there, the warm climate that suited B.-P.'s old bones, the magnificent view of Mount Kenya, the 'Treetops' hide (now so famous) from which B.-P. could watch and paint the wild creatures he loved.

They had a bungalow built at Nyeri with the intention of spending each winter there. They moved into 'Paxtu', as it was called, in November 1938 intending to return to England the following summer, but B.-P. was not fit enough to make the journey. The outbreak of hostilities had precluded any chance of returning to England.

For a while, in the gentle climate of Kenya, his health improved and he spent his time writing and painting. Some of his best work is a series of water-colours of wild life painted in the last year of his life and published as *Birds and Beasts in Africa* and *More Sketches of Kenya*.

In September 1940, however, he had a relapse. The doctor warned his wife that his heart was 'awfully tired'. The life that had been so packed with action and ideas and ideals was slowly ebbing away. He had had the satisfaction of living to see his three children grown up and happily married; to watch the two great Movements that he had founded grow in strength and influence. He had found the woman of his dreams and had enjoyed her loving support for nearly thirty years. It was time to go.

On Christmas Day, 1940, he sat out of bed to listen to the King's broadcast speech to the Empire; on January 6th, 1941, he was just conscious enough to nod in understanding when his wife gave him the news of an Italian defeat at Bardia; then he just slipped into a coma and on January 8th, 1941, the great heart that had spread so much happiness throughout the world stopped beating. He was almost eighty-four.

They buried his body in a simple grave at Nyeri, within sight of Mount Kenya. Soldiers and Scouts, white and black, escorted the coffin to its last resting-place. But that was only the mortal frame. His spirit lives on today, wherever there are Scouts.

In spite of our boasted civilisation and in spite of two thousand years of Christianity, we have gained as yet but a veneer of civilisation [he wrote], and the Christianity which we profess is not that which we really practise in our lives and actions. Self-interest and mistrust rule the world.

The only sound basis on which to build is the spirit of love and goodwill among people in the place of mutual jealousies and mistrust. This can only be secured by bringing up the next generation in a changed outlook.

This sounds like a Utopian dream and might reasonably be laughed out of court were it not that the Boy Scout and Girl Guide movement has shown that it should not be impossible.

I don't pretend that they alone can bring it about — but they can help . . .

How many men and women have been Scouts and Guides since the beginning of the century is impossible to estimate — the numbers must run into hundreds of millions. Shortly before he died, B.-P. said, 'When the numbers of Scouts comprise millions of men in our population, all in touch with the Movement and with each other, and all actuated by the Scout spirit of goodwill and service, what will it not mean for the loyalty and steadfastness of a solid proportion of the nation?'

Since that day thirty odd years ago when B.-P. 'went home', Scouting has moved to even greater strengths. There are now some fourteen million Scouts and eight million Guides throughout the world. This has come about not just through

Lady Baden-Powell's tireless work — for she has served both Scouting and Guiding with unflagging loyalty throughout her widowhood — but also because Scouting still has as much to offer the modern boy as it did at the beginning of the century. The details may have changed slightly over the years. The uniform is more 'uniform'; the programme caters for the more sophisticated tastes of the nineteen-seventies. That is as B.-P. would have wished it. 'The world is changing,' he wrote in a memo to Headquarters from one of his Canadian tours. 'Evolution is going on all around us. We must keep *au fait* with this; and by looking around and looking wide and looking ahead we must see in what line we can progress and be ahead rather than behind the times.'

But the essentials of Scouting have not changed; its trust in God and its dedication to service have not changed — those essentials that B.-P. summed up in a last message that was found among his papers after he had died:

Dear Scouts, — if you have ever seen the play *Peter Pan* you will remember how the pirate chief was always making his dying speech because he was afraid that possibly when the time came for him to die he might not have time to get it off his chest. It is much the same with me, and so, although I am not at this moment dying, I shall be doing so one of these days and I want to send you a parting word of goodbye.

Remember, it is the last you will ever hear from me, so think it over.

I have had a most happy life and I want each one of you to have as happy a life too.

I believe that God put us in this jolly world to be happy and enjoy life. Happiness doesn't come from being rich, nor merely from being successful in your career, nor by self-indulgence. One step towards happiness is to make yourself healthy and strong while you are a boy, so that you can *be useful* and so can enjoy life when you are a man.

Nature study will show you how full of beautiful and wonderful things God has made the world for you to enjoy. Be contented with what you have got and make the best of it. Look on the bright side of things instead of the gloomy one.

But the real way to get happiness is by giving out happiness to other people. Try and leave this world a little better than you found it and when your turn comes to die, you can die happy in feeling that at any rate you have not wasted your time but have *done your best*. 'Be Prepared' in this way, to live happy and to die happy — stick to your Scout promise always — even after you have ceased to be a boy — and God help you to do it.

Your Friend,

BADEN-POWELL

The Scout sign
meaning
'I have gone home'
which is on the headstone
of B.-P.'s grave
at Nyeri, Kenya.

B.-P.'s Honours and Awards

1901   Companion of the Order of the Bath
1909   Knight Commander of the Order of the Bath
       Knight Commander of the Victorian Order
1910   Order of Merit of Chile
1912   Knight of Grace of St. John of Jerusalem
1919   Knight of the Grand Cross of Alfonso XII (Spain)
1920   Grand Commander of the Order of Christ (Portugal)
       Grand Commander of the Order of the Redeemer (Greece)
1921   Created Baronet
       Storkos of the Order of Danneborg (Denmark)
       Order of the Commander of the Crown of Belgium
1922   Commander of the Legion of Honour (France)
1923   Grand Cross of the Victorian Order
1927   Order of Polonia Restituta (Poland)
1928   Knight Grand Cross of the Order of St. Michael and St. George
       Order of Amanulla (Afghanistan)
1929   First Class of the Order of Merit (Hungary)
       The Order of the White Lion (Czechoslovakia)
       The Order of the Phoenix (Greece)
       Created Baron Baden-Powell of Gilwell
1931   The Grand Cross of the Order of Merit (Austria)
1932   Grand Cross of Gediminus (Lithuania)
       Grand Cross of Orange of Nassau (Holland)
1933   Commander of the Order of the Oak of Luxembourg
       The Red Cross of Estonia
       Grand Cross of the Order of the Sword (Sweden)
1936   Grand Cordon of the Legion of Honour (France)
1937   Wateler Peace Prize
       Order of Merit

HONORARY DEGREES

1910	LL.D	Edinburgh
1923	LL.D	Toronto
	LL.D	McGill, Montreal
	D.C.L.	Oxford
1929	LL.D.	Liverpool
1931	LL.D.	Cambridge